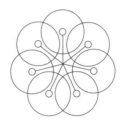

The Sound of Healing
UNVEILING THE PHENOMENA
OF *WHOLETONES*

BY MICHAEL S. TYRRELL

The Sound of Healing: Unveiling the Phenomena of Wholetones
by Michael S. Tyrrell
Second Edition: November 2015
ISBN (paperback): 978-0-692-29197-9
ISBN (hardcover): 9 780996 746021

Printed in the United States of America
Published & Distributed by Barton Publishing
Barton Publishing PO Box 50 Brandon, SD 57005
BartonPublishing.com 1-888-356-1146

Copy Editor: Cheryl Ravey, Linda Rohrbaugh, and Taty Vilaplana
Spanish Version Translated by Taty Vilaplana
Layout by Joel Harrison at AlbumArtDesign.com
Additional Content by Joel Harrison, Marty Fahncke, and Linda
Rohrbaugh

does mention of specific companies, organizations, or authorities imply that they endorse this book, its author, or the publisher. Internet address or telephone numbers given in this book were accurate at the time it went to press.

Special Sales: *Wholetones* books are available at special discounts for bulk purchases for sales promotions or premiums. For further information or permission, write to Lillian Tyrrell at Lillian@MichaelTyrrell.com or visit www.MichaelTyrrell.com

"Wholetones" and "Chroma" are trademarks of Michael Tyrrell Music, LLC.

Visit wholetones.com to purchase *Wholetones* music, videos, and to learn more.

VI

Dedication

I dedicate this book to God,
the Father of Lights,
the Creator of Sound & Frequency,
and the Architect of Heaven & Earth.

Contents

x

Endorsements

"Michael Tyrrell is one of those people who makes you feel like royalty when you're around him. He is filled with the love of God and has a powerful understanding of Jesus and His kingdom. We have traveled the world together and it is very evident to me that Michael is carrying a special piece of what is needed in this generation. He is an authentic expression of love who imparts hope everywhere he goes. I have learned a lot from Michael and I'm happy to call him a friend."

RICK PINO
The Heart of David
www.rickpino.com

"I met Michael and Lillian Tyrrell in 2007 after being a Christian for 2 years. They have poured their heart and soul into my life.

A strong deliverance took place in me while Michael performed his song, Lion In The Garden. Michael has a real heart for the church to walk in freedom and maturity. I'm proud to call him and Lillian my friends."

BRIAN WELCH
Korn
iamsecond.com/seconds/brian-welch

"It has been my great privilege to know Michael Tyrrell throughout the years. I've found him to be kind, direct, loving, and a great prophetic voice to our church.

It's my honor to endorse the author of this book!"

Pastor Kirk Gilchrist
New Life Christian Church, Watertown, New York
www.newlifenny.com

"As a worshiper, one of my expectant hopes is what the Prophet Amos first writes and reaffirmed in the Book of Acts: the Restoration of the Tabernacle of David. A hunger for a deeper worship experience leads me to sense that David's Tabernacle is more about a coming level of worship, rather than the rebuilding of a physical structure. I believe the restoration of the Tabernacle of David cannot be complete without the Key of David.

No doubt in this season, God has imparted to Michael Tyrrell that key. A twofold key, one that not only unlocks doors, but a musical key that defines the healing qualities of Heaven's tonic chords as given by God to David and rediscovered in Divine epiphany by Michael. This revelation will define healing for this generation."

MICHAEL COLEMAN
Pastor
Oviedo, Florida

"Once in a while you meet one of those souls that just by being in near proximity to them, your whole day seems to get a lot brighter. Michael is one of those souls. His presence and his laughter can make the dullest of places seem like an extraordinary festivity. His kind heart and deep understanding of the spiritual realm gives anyone in need refuge and comfort.

We are all grateful to our creator for giving us an Amazing Earth Angel named Michael Tyrrell. Thank you Michael for all you do to make our world a better place."

DR. SHINO BAY AGUILERA
Board Certified Dermatologist & Dermatologic Surgeon, Physician Trainer & Clinical Researcher

Foreword

When I first met Michael, I was intrigued by his long hair and charismatic personality. He was like "Rockstar Jesus" who loved to talk about the Kingdom of God in a way I had never heard before. Five years later, I am honored to call him one of my closest friends.

Michael's zest for life, his quest for truth, his love for God, and his passion for sharing the kingdom with others energizes and encourages me greatly.

I've had the privilege of working closely with Michael since February 2014 to help bring one of his dreams to life, and I'm honored to contribute to the work of **Wholetones: The Sound of Healing.**

Others have called this project Michael's magnum opus, the pinnacle of his life's work and possibly the very reason he was created.

But I see this as an outpouring of love inspired from the depth of his soul that has been imprinted on his DNA and is now available for you to experience and enjoy forever.

In fact, when I listen to the music of *Wholetones* (which is quite often, including right now as I write), I cannot help but feel that this music is going to be resonating in the halls of Heaven for all eternity. And we get to listen to it right here, right now. That's pretty cool.

I'd like to share two very personal stories about *Wholetones* that I experienced before we launched *Wholetones* together.

First, I wasn't able to attend the studio recording of the music – but I was greatly anticipating hearing the songs once they were finished. Michael called me with updates, talking about how he couldn't believe how everything was coming together so smoothly. He didn't write any of the music ahead of time … he just trusted that it would come as the Spirit led. The musicians came to the studio not really knowing what to expect. Michael spent much time in prayer, and when it was time to record, the music flowed out like the birthing of a newborn baby, and they could only explain the entire project as divinely inspired.

A few days after they finished recording, he sent me a "secret link" to the music. So I plugged my phone into my home stereo system, downloaded the song, pressed play, and listened. What I heard was simply amazing. I stood in my living room and wept. I danced, I laughed, and I praised God. It was a deeply spiritual moment for me that I will never forget. The music was beautiful, and I knew it was going to make a transformational difference in so many people's lives.

My next story is about my mother. She had been suffering with stage IV breast cancer that spread to her bones since 2009. In December 2013, she was looking and feeling great. But in January, her health took a turn for the worse and when we visited with her on Easter, she had lost a lot of weight and was very frail and weak. We cried a lot together as we knew she was dying and we both felt the pain. I remember stroking her thin hair while she laid in her bed, as I know she used to stroke my hair when I was a small child.

Before it was time to leave, I played song 741Hz, Great Awakening, on her iPad, and we listened to it together in her living room. After two minutes, she looked over at me to see how I was doing, because she was crying. I was balling and snot was draining from my nose like a babbling baby. The music penetrated to our souls and helped us feel like everything was going to be alright, even though her earthly tent was withering away.

My mother went to be with her Lord Jesus Christ on 12/13/2014, and thankfully she is no longer suffering with any pain, frailty, or weakness. My sister just suffered a very early term miscarriage, but we both agree that her baby is now snuggling in the arms of Ma, close to Jesus, waiting for us to get there. This music continues to help us heal from the emotional pain of losing someone close. My dad tells me he listens to *Wholetones* every night, and it's helped him through the grieving process.

One thing I am most looking forward to is hearing the stories that will come from people like you after listening to and absorbing this music into your life. Spontaneous healings, mended relationships, increased productivity, vibrant health, spawning of creative ideas, and a general sense of calm and peace are just some of the benefits that I have personally witnessed or experienced, and I know others will too.

And I give all the glory to the Lord Jesus Christ, because ultimately, this is another of His amazing gifts to us. I pray you feel His presence in your life today and believe on His name to get you through any trial or tribulation you may be facing in your life.

So sit back, put on some good headphones, press play, and allow God to use these healing sounds to minister to you at a deep level. Enjoy each song as the music dances effortlessly and resonates to the core of your being.

JOE BARTON
Founder & CEO, Barton Publishing, Inc.
jb@bartonpublishing.com

Preface

How can a truth seeker stop until the truth is revealed?
—**Michael Tyrrell**

When I started writing this book I had no idea that it would literally take on a life of its own. It has pulled from every experience of my life and stretched me as a writer, revelator, musician, minister, and husband.

During the writing, I also recorded *Wholetones* by divine inspiration in Dallas, Texas. *Wholetones* is a 7 CD set with each track running 22:22 minutes. This project took 7 days to record and mix, and ended on Passover! And much like the book, the recording project tapped everything I had physically, emotionally, and spiritually.

The first indicator that the music captured something otherworldly was my wife's initial response to the recordings. Lillian is a great sounding board for anything I create because she is unapologetically honest. This time she was honestly overwhelmed, as were the few people I allowed to audit the pre-release.

As a seasoned musician I am accustomed to critique. Historically, some of my projects have reminded people of various or different bands. But for the first time in my life, everyone who listened to this recording project said the exact same thing:

"This is unbelievable! I have never heard anything like it."

And rightly so! *Wholetones* is a live, spontaneous recording in a key that hasn't been heard in centuries!

Both the book and the recording project demanded an upside down approach. The songs and the book title were the last things to come instead of the first!

Truthfully, when I arrived at the recording studio and looked into the faces of the amazing musicians I had asked to join me, I felt very inept. I knew they were looking for direction or lead sheets ... or something! But I had nothing. So I told them I was going to sit and listen to 7 frequencies on the headphones until I heard the music we were to play. Then, and only then, I would tell them what to do. The result is the *Wholetones* music 7 CD set that many of you received with this book!

I am convinced that you will never know up front when you are creating your "magnum opus," or life's work. It usually comes as a complete surprise. Those of us who are creative are often far too close to our own creations to see them for what they are worth.

But let me clue you in. You probably don't realize how long you have been carrying the bulk of the information in your heart. For 15, 18, 24 years it may have been hidden away within you. But, suddenly, it pours out of you like a pent-up stream, filling the pages of a book and 7 audio CDs which can be found on www.wholetones.com.

I never would have considered just how much weight this project carries until someone I trust said to me, "This project may be the reason you were created." Now, THAT is a heavy thought.

As you begin this book, I would ask that you read it not as a distant fiction novel or heady scientific resource. If so, you may just find yourself hidden between its pages. I wrote this book for reluctant pioneers, closet revolutionaries, unsung heroes, undecorated champions, faint saints, poets who don't know it, unknown musicians, writers, sculptors, painters, and underdogs of all sorts. I wrote this book for you!

Sometimes the luggage of life paralyzes and the long wait mesmerizes one into the belief that your time will never come. Friend, you've been hidden for a reason for just the perfect season. And before you know it, your anonymity will find its voice! Here's to the sunrise of your obscurity ... and mine as well!

MICHAEL S. TYRRELL
Founder & CEO, Wholetones, Inc.
http://www.michaeltyrrell.com

CHAPTER 1:
The Game Changers

Since the beginning of time there have been people who challenged the status quo. Their pioneering spirits have led to some of the greatest discoveries and accomplishments in history.

These pioneers often overcame ridicule, controversy, frustration, and seemingly insurmountable odds. But their great personal sacrifice has opened a window large enough for all of us to see the unseen and know the unknown.

Although this pioneering spirit has existed since the beginning, the Renaissance period was amazingly rife with game changers and iconoclasts.

A brief look at just a few of these amazing renaissance men and their accomplishments will help you understand the impetus behind this guide and the recordings you hold in your hand.

MARTIN LUTHER (1483-1546)
Theologian, Augustinian monk, author, musician, & reformer
https://en.wikipedia.org/wiki/Martin_Luther

Luther was undoubtedly the central figure of the Protestant Reformation. He brazenly challenged the corrupt Roman religious system. Luther taught that salvation and eternal life were not earned by good deeds or purchasing indulgences. Instead, you receive salvation only as a free gift of God's grace through faith in Jesus Christ.

Luther believed that the Word of God was for everyone, not just the aristocracy. On October 31st, 1517, Luther nailed his famous 95 theses to the church door at Wittenberg, Germany, accusing the Roman Catholic Church of heresy upon heresy. This act was the tipping point of the Protestant Reformation.

Luther's controversial and ground-breaking theological works eventually led to his excommunication. In a divine twist of fate, this act afforded Luther the time to translate the Bible from Latin into German, the language of his people. His translation of the Bible influenced the English translation known as the Tyndale Bible.[1]

Luther was also a gifted musician. His hymns influenced corporate singing in church. In fact, his hymns are still sung today in churches throughout the world.

Yes, one diminutive monk turned the religious system upside down, or shall we say ... right side up!

CHRISTOPHER COLUMBUS (1451-1506)
Explorer, navigator, & colonizer
https://en.wikipedia.org/wiki/Christopher_Columbus

After his wife Filipa died, Christopher Columbus moved to Spain with his son, Diego, and began a series of attempts to obtain a grant to explore western trade routes.

Columbus firmly believed the earth's shape was spherical. But, the educated in Europe feared they would fall off the edge of the earth because it was flat. So with great criticism, his request for a grant to prove his theory was flatly denied on several occasions.

Undaunted in his resolve, Columbus found favor with Queen Isabella. In 1492, he promised to bring back gold, spices, and silk from Asia, spread Christianity, and explore China. King Ferdinand and Queen Isabella gave Columbus his grant, and made him admiral of the seas and governor of discovered lands.

Although Columbus never reached Asia or North America, his voyages marked the colonization of the American continents. And, of course, proved once and for all that the earth was anything but flat.

LEONARDO DA VINCI (1452-1519)
Italian Renaissance sage, painter, sculptor, architect, musician, mathematician, engineer, inventor, anatomist, geologist, cartographer, botanist, & writer.
https://en.wikipedia.org/wiki/Leonardo_da_Vinci

Probably more than any other, Leonardo da Vinci was the epitome of the Renaissance man. He was filled with an unquenchable curiosity and a non-stop capacity for invention.

He is considered one of the greatest painters of all time. Among Leonardo da Vinci's works are the Mona Lisa, the Last Supper, and the iconic drawing, the Vitruvian Man.

As far as inventors go, Leonardo was unrivaled. He blueprinted flying machines, a tank, split hull boats, adding machines, and concentrated solar power. He also theorized plate tectonics. Although his larger inventions were not feasible for construction in his time, he built an automated bobbin winder and a machine to measure the tensile strength of wire.[2]

Leonardo was also responsible for important discoveries in anatomy, optics, and hydrodynamics. You may have heard the old maxim, "Jack of all trades; master of none." Well, Leonardo da Vinci mastered all that he undertook.

NICOLAUS COPERNICUS (1473-1543)
Renaissance mathematician & astronomer who formulated
a heliocentric (sun-centered) model of the universe.
https://en.wikipedia.org/wiki/Nicolaus_Copernicus

Copernicus was a revolutionary in the truest sense of the word. His writing, *On the Revolutions of the Celestial Spheres*, earned him a place in history. He proved that planets revolve around the sun and disproved Ptolemy's claim that the sun revolved around the planets.

Drawing the Lines of Commonality

All of the aforementioned Renaissance men and their contemporaries had several significant attributes in common that allowed them to succeed where others had failed. Here are a few notable ones:

1. All of them believed that laws represented uncertainty and could therefore be broken. Jodocus Trutfetter, one of Martin Luther's tutors, taught him to be suspicious of even the greatest thinkers and to test everything himself by experience. Luther was certainly unconventional in his thoughts!

2. All of them were free of the fear of man, yet viewed God with great awe.

3. All of them were highly educated. Most spoke several languages and possessed a high degree of proficiency in mathematics and the arts, as well as a variety of other skills.

4. All of them pursued life with passion and fierce tenacity. Unrelenting in their search for truth, they NEVER gave up.

5. Historians often labeled Renaissance men humanistic.[2] But closer inspection of their altruistic behavior proves they also valued benevolence, faith, and revelation. After all, the spiritual reformation that accompanied the reformation of the arts, science, and literature was obviously not perpetuated by human means.

6. The Renaissance Christian saw creation in perfect order, from God down to the most insignificant creature or object. They

saw creation as an act of imposing divine organization upon raw chaos. The popular thought interpreted was closer to orderliness is next to godliness.

"In the Beginning, God created the Heavens and the earth. The earth was without form, and darkness was upon the face of the deep: and the Spirit of God moved over the waters."
† Genesis 1:1-2 ESV

They saw the divine order, or chain of authority, as follows:[2]

- God, the Creator, is the highest link
  in the chain, yet outside of it.

- Purely spiritual beings were below the Creator.

- Beings of both spirit and physical body (human
  beings) were below angelic beings.

- Animate creatures with only physical bodies
  and five senses, but lacking reason (mammals,
  fowl, fish, and insects), followed next.

- Animals with fewer than five senses or inanimate bodies
  (oysters, mollusks, barnacles, etc.) were next in line.

- Then plant life, which is inanimate and
  without sensory capabilities (trees, shrubs,
  vegetables), continued the chain of order.

- Finally, minerals and inanimate objects
  were the lowest elements.

7. Humanist Renaissance men saw this information as:
    - The basis for survival of the fittest

    - The food chain

    - The four elements (fire, air, water, earth)

They also saw this transformation from the lens of alchemy, rather than divinity.

There is one thing virtually all Renaissance men agreed on: there is infinitely more to creation than meets the eye or the intellect and it MUST be discovered at all cost!

Your Own Personal Renaissance

As you read on, you will discover that man's innate need for control has been the impetus behind his attempts to measure time, space, and history. Needless to say, these attempts have often been extremely inaccurate and should always be challenged.

Do you remember pictures of cavemen in your school history books? There were also pictures of the caveman's environment, tools and weapons, and dietary habits. This was all unapologetically taught to young impressionable children as truth. But was it the TRUTH?

In man's pursuit of making a monkey out of himself, he created the following elaborate hoaxes to establish a "missing link" that would prove Darwin's theory of evolution.[3]

- Java Man (a coffee lover … just kidding!) was created from random bones not even associated with each other. But a deathbed confession from the archaeologist who created the hoax (I mean, "discovered the caveman") admitted that the scull cap came from a gibbon (ape)!

- Peking Man (fossils from China) was said to be 400,000 years old. Yet after the remains were "lost" during WWII, his age was suddenly changed to 350,000-500,000 years old. Now, that's quite a stretch! Later scientists confirmed that the Peking Man was just a modern man merely a few thousand years young.

- Nebraska Man was a man built from nothing more than a tooth. In fact, it was the same tooth that Clarence Darrow held up as evidence of human evolution in the Scopes trial of 1925. In 1927, scientists took a closer look at the tooth and realized it belonged to a pig! Yes indeed, the entire story was a pig in a poke. That's the tooth, the whole tooth, and nothing but … the tooth.

- The Piltdown Man, when first found, was thought to be 500,000 years old. But researchers discovered that someone deliberately planted 500 and 600 year old bones with the skull to try and prove evolution. Further investigation only proved the Piltdown man to be another hoax.

- Lack of evidence resulted in the conclusion that Heidelberg Man was a modern species.

- Neanderthal Man was a forgery, ultimately proven to be a modern species.

- Like all other theories relating to early man, Cro-Magnon Man has not yet been proven to be anything but a modern species.

So, why are these lies still being purported as truth today? Why is the propagation of a theory into a truth such a common occurrence? Why is the theory of evolution so important? In a word, PRIDE! Man hates to admit it when he is in error and creates elaborate hoaxes, historical distortions, and cultural chaos instead of admitting defeat.

Here is something I want you to consider. If you look at the birth years of the aforementioned Renaissance men, do you see a correlation? The works of several renowned historians do not agree on a date when the Renaissance period started or ended.[6] So, they adopted the 1400-1700 AD time span.

Let me get this straight. The evolutionists studying dead bones have had to modify their theories once again. Humans studying humans base an important time in history on the birthdates of some enlightened people who lived and died in a certain period of time?

It is time to challenge everything you think you know and dare to discover the truth. The Renaissance isn't a period of time as much as it is a "state" of being. It is far more about WHO you are than WHERE you are in time.

Enlightened people, not time, create their own renaissance. Renaissance can break out anytime or anywhere. You may be one of these enlightened ones and not even be aware of it! By the way, Renaissance defined means rebirth, revival, or "coming around" as one who was unconscious.[7] This book is your smelling salts. Wake up!

CHAPTER 2:
Proximity vs. Perspective

Now *let me ask* you a few questions …

- How many of the Renaissance attributes mentioned above do you possess? What (or who) motivated you to purchase the resource you now hold in your hand?

- Are you one who unquestioningly accepts as fact what culture dictates as the absolute truth?

- Is reality relative?

The word "proximity" is defined as nearness in space, time, or relationship.

The word "perspective" has this definition: The way YOU see something, your point of view.

Proximity is where you actually are and perspective is where you think you are. If you look at the side view mirror of your car you will find an indelibly scripted warning, "Objects in the mirror are closer than they appear." Car manufacturers place that warning there because the mirror is slightly concave. This creates an imperfect perspective, or point of view, regarding distance. If you trust that perspective, then when you change lanes the proximity of the car you hit invalidates your perspective! Remember, proximity always trumps perspective.

Life is far more than meets the eye. For example, let's say you are standing on a street corner in Manhattan and you are facing a tall building. All you can see from your vantage point is the tall building, so you assume it takes up the entire corner. Yet just above you, at the same street corner, a man in a helicopter sees a tall thin building on the corner with lots of little buildings behind it. Just because you didn't see the other buildings had no bearing on the fact of their existence.

Now you cross the street and enter the tall building. You are surprised that it only has an 8-foot ceiling, but you quickly accept what you see as reality. When you ask the janitor why such a tall building has an 8-foot ceiling he replies, "This building has a 50 ft. ceiling. The 8-foot ceiling you see is a drop ceiling. What you didn't see is the 42 feet of storage just above the ceiling tiles."

A Renaissance man, would have grabbed a broom, knocked out one of the ceiling tiles and exclaimed, "Eureka, I knew there was more!"

That is the difference between a linear thinker and a non-linear thinker. Let me define them for you.[8]

Linear thinking: "To look at something from one point of view."

Nonlinear thinking: "To look at something from several, often unrelated points of view."

Most of our thinking is linear or "logical." We consider this to be normal, conventional thinking. But the Renaissance men didn't just think in a linear way. The world's biggest game changers have always tried new and innovative approaches for generating ideas, accessing knowledge and discovery.

If you haven't figured it out yet, this resource is FAR more than an instruction book and seven CDs. It is a key to your self-discovery. Self-discovery, or "Nosce Te Ipsum" Latin for "To know thyself," is the first step to healing and personal transformation. Without this knowledge of our identity and human condition, we would never discover our need (and ability) to be healed or transformed.

"For as he thinks in his heart, so is he."

† Proverbs 23:7 AMP

The Narrow Way

> **"Enter through the narrow gate. For wide is the gate
> and broad is the road that leads to destruction, and
> many enter through it. But small is the gate and nar-
> row the road that leads to life, and only a few find it."**
> † *Matthew 7:13-14*

In 1964, Rankin/Bass released a Christmas television special aired on the NBC network entitled, "Rudolf the Red-Nosed Reindeer."[9] Response to the show was overwhelming and it has remained a cult classic to this day. The Island of Misfit Toys scene struck a nerve with many viewers. They wrote the network asking that they include a scene with Santa rescuing the misfits. NBC graciously agreed and added that scene. After I list some of the misfits you will immediately understand the reason I mentioned them in this book.

- King Moonracer, the winged Lion that rules the Island

- Charlie-In-The-Box

- The Spotted Elephant

- Dolly, a seemingly normal toy doll
  discarded by her mistress and suffering
  from depression from being unloved

- A bird who swims instead of flies

- A cowboy who rides an ostrich

- A train with square wheels

- A boat that cannot float

- An airplane that cannot fly

- And a water pistol that shoots jelly

Have you ever felt like a misfit? Are you often misunderstood? Are you pistachio in a chocolate and vanilla world? Have you found it easier to disdain your gift than to celebrate it?

Right now you must be thinking, "A gift? What gift?"

Yes you are a priceless gift, a rare commodity in the midst of conformity. Your loving Creator meticulously designed you this way. You see, King Moonracer is a Christ type, a loving king who watched over and protected his misfits. Though the world saw them as flawed and useless, he knew them as the wonders they truly were.

Begin right now to be thankful for who you are and LOVE yourself and the ONE who made you this way. Next time you look in a mirror, take an extra minute to really examine each amazing characteristic that you possess – what makes you uniquely you. Before long you will realize that you are one of a kind, like a snowflake, and dearly loved.

"For you created my inmost being; you knit me together in my mother's womb. I praise you because I am fearfully and wonderfully made; your works are wonderful, I know that full well."
† Psalm 139:13-14

Although the road you are on may seem uphill, narrow, and sparsely traveled, in the end you will be glad you followed your inner voice instead of the jeering crowd. And in bypassing the compass of conformity (magnetic north), you will soon discover TRUE north!

CHAPTER 3:
Time & Eternity

O ne of the most difficult things for humans to grasp is the immense difference between time and eternity. Since a rudimentary knowledge of this subject will be necessary in our understanding of how frequencies work, let's spend a moment deciphering the differences.

- Time is finite

- Eternity is infinite

- Time is linear

- Eternity is non-linear

- Time is a straight line

- Eternity is a circle

Consider the terms, "beginning of time," "end of time," and "fullness of time," in contrast to eternity which does not possess a beginning or an end and is full or complete entirely in and of itself.

Here is an illustration to help you see the difference. Let's say that one grain of sand from an hourglass represents time and the Sahara desert represents eternity. Now drop that grain of sand (time) into the Sahara desert (eternity) and you get the picture. Where did all the time go? Eternity exists outside of time, but time does not exist outside of eternity. Eternity never began and it never ends, yet time has a beginning and an end. Thus eternity swallows time whole! Time is a unit of measure; eternity is immeasurable.

To even enter the vestibule of understanding so great a mystery, we need to grasp that man's attempt to accurately measure time is an epic failure. Carbon 14 testing that supposedly predicts the accurate age of dinosaur bones has also tested living organisms and declared them dead for millions of years.[10] Today, an hour represents 60 minutes. But that was NOT the case in ancient times. Measured "sun time" and "clock time" are different.

Sun time is based on the sun reaching its highest point (the meridian) in the middle of the day and reaching its highest point on the next day to complete a full cycle. However, the time between the Sun reaching its successive meridians is quite often different than clock time.

In actuality, a day is close to 24 hours from May to August. Yet in late October, days are about 15 minutes shorter. In mid-February, the days are about 14 minutes longer. Because of man's scheduling of events, we MUST keep a consistent clock time of 24 hours.

By the time you factor in the myriads of different calendars used over centuries, leap years, daylight savings time, the earth's rotational changes, and fuzzy math, one obvious conclusion remains.[11] Much to our surprise (and wounded pride), we don't have a clue what time it is, what day it is, or even what YEAR it is!

And next time you have a little time on your hands (sorry!), stare intently at the second hand of your wristwatch. Usually within five minutes you will see something extraordinary. Your second hand will quickly tick backward for a nanosecond before continuing forward. Congratulations, that little second hand hiccup you witnessed is a schism in man's flawed measurement of time. With that in mind, before we continue, meditate on this verse in 2 Peter 3:8.

> "But DO NOT forget this one thing, dear
> friends: With the Lord a day is like a thou-
> sand years, and a thousand years like a day."
> † 2 Peter 3:8

The book of Genesis records the six-day creation story. In chapter one, on day ONE God said, "Let there be light" and there WAS light. And God saw that the light was good and He separated the light from the darkness. (This makes a "nightlight" an oxymoron!) God called the light "day" and the darkness He called "night" and both of these existed on the FIRST day. (Genesis 1:3-5) Now the fun begins.

And God said, "Let there be lights in the expanse of the sky to SEPARATE the day from the night, and let them serve as signs to mark seasons and days and years, and let them be lights in the expanse of the sky to give light ON THE EARTH. And it was so. God made two great lights-the greater light to govern the day and the lesser to govern the night. He also made the stars. God set them in the expanse of the sky to give light on the earth, to govern the day and the night, and to separate light from darkness. And God saw that it was good. And there was evening, and there was morning, THE FOURTH DAY." (Genesis 1:14-19, emphasis mine)

Did you see it? On day ONE, God said, "Let there be light," and there WAS light. If God didn't create the sun, moon, and stars until day four, then where did the light come from? Keep reading! The answers are coming!

On day four, the lights (sun, moon, and stars) in the expanse of the sky gave light on the earth and served as signs to MARK seasons and days and years. This is what man calls time. Time is a measured or "marked" subdivision in eternity that was initially measured by creating sundials and calendars. This eventually evolved into a clock face. Now, let's take the time to have a bit more fun.

You see, in man's need for control he often takes liberties that quickly become fallacies purported as absolutes. Being so marinated in linear thinking since birth, man continues to build upon these assumptions for generations. All the while, man perpetuates nothing more than a popular belief gone rogue. To illustrate this point, let's look at a poem by Sam Walter Foss entitled, *The Calf Path*.[12]

I.

One day, through the primeval wood,
A calf walked home, as good calves should;

II.

But made a trail all bent askew,
A crooked trail as all calves do.
Since then three hundred years have fled,
And, I infer, the calf is dead.
But still he left behind his trail,
And thereby hangs my moral tale.
The trail was taken up next day,
By a lone dog that passed that way.
And then a wise bell-wether sheep,

Pursued the trail o'er vale and steep;
And drew the flock behind him too,
As good bell-wethers always do.
And from that day, o'er hill and glade.
Through those old woods a path was made.

III.

And many men wound in and out,
And dodged, and turned, and bent about;
And uttered words of righteous wrath,
Because 'twas such a crooked path.
But still they followed - do not laugh -
The first migrations of that calf.
And through this winding wood-way stalked,
Because he wobbled when he walked.

IV.

This forest path became a lane,
That bent, and turned, and turned again.
This crooked lane became a road,
Where many a poor horse with his load,
Toiled on beneath the burning sun,
And traveled some three miles in one.
And thus a century and a half,
They trod the footsteps of that calf.

V.

The years passed on in swiftness fleet,
The road became a village street;
And this, before men were aware,
A city's crowded thoroughfare;
And soon the central street was this,
Of a renowned metropolis;

And men two centuries and a half,
Trod in the footsteps of that calf.

VI.

Each day a hundred thousand rout,
Followed the zigzag calf about;
And o'er his crooked journey went,
The traffic of a continent.
A Hundred thousand men were led,
By one calf near three centuries dead.
They followed still his crooked way,
And lost one hundred years a day;
For thus such reverence is lent,
To well established precedent.

VII.

A moral lesson this might teach,
Were I ordained and called to preach;
For men are prone to go it blind,
Along the calf-paths of the mind;
And work away from sun to sun,
To do what other men have done.
They follow in the beaten track,
And out and in, and forth and back,
And still their devious course pursue,
To keep the path that others do.
They keep the path a sacred groove,
Along which all their lives they move.
But how the wise old wood gods laugh,
Who saw the first primeval calf!
Ah! Many things this tale might teach -
But I am not ordained to preach.

Isn't that the way of the world? Follow the leader no matter how crooked and corrupt his path may be and dare never question it!

Now you have to ask yourself another tough question. How much information passed down throughout history reported as absolute truth is actually fiction, fable, or fantasy? It is commonly known that stories passed down through generations are often embellished and important details are often omitted or forgotten. By the time it reaches your ears it may have lost something in its translation.

I will make you this promise. I am basing the information shared with you in this book on confirmed scientific, historic, and biblical fact. If a statement is personal revelation or legend, I will bring that to your attention.

When surveyors are measuring they first must lay a benchmark. A benchmark is a fixed position of reference precisely known as the starting point. If the benchmark is accurate, then the job will be accurate. If it is off, then the job will more than likely be off.

Likewise, if you were lost in the desert and all you had to navigate your way out was a compass and your calculations were off by just one degree, then you could end up hundreds of miles from your objective. Remember the narrow way is a direct route and the broad road is just … a calf path.

Now that I have slaughtered many of history's "Sacred Cows" in the valley of the misinformed, it is time for us to ascend the mountain of revelation.

CHAPTER 4:
Freakquency or Frequency

Everything emits frequency. A frequency is a measured point of a vibration or energy. Everything possesses a resonant frequency. "Resonance is the phenomenon that occurs when a physical system is periodically disturbed at the same period of one of its natural frequencies."[13]

Think of it as transmitting and receiving.

For example, if a guitar string is vibrating at the frequency 440 Hz, then you will hear the note A.

Now if the resonant frequency of the guitar itself is 440 Hz, then every time you hit the A string (also 440 Hz) the whole guitar will shake!

When this matching of frequencies occurs, we call it sympathetic resonance. Here is my working definition.

"Sympathetic resonance or sympathetic vibration is a harmonic phenomenon wherein a formerly passive string or vibratory body responds to external vibrations to which it has a harmonic likeness."

When sharing a thought, you might have heard this response, "That really resonates with me" or "I feel you." In essence, when there is an identically shared thought or feeling with another person, this is sympathetic resonance manifesting. And it is powerful.

You can probably recall times when you instantly felt a common bond or connection with someone you just met and immediately enjoyed being around that person. Likewise, you may remember meeting someone and couldn't get away from them fast enough. Scientists have a big word for this exchange of positive or negative non-verbal information: limbic resonance or vibration.

To illustrate my point, let me take you back to October of 1966. The Beach Boys have just released their hit single, Good Vibrations. Let's look at the lyrics of the chorus.[14]

"I'm pickin' up good vibrations (good, good, good, good vibrations) ... She's giving me excitations."

In other words, one person is detecting good vibrations because another person is sending good vibrations. Plus, the one receiving them is excited! This is a perfect explanation of naturally occurring phenomena. Energy is transmitted; energy is received and energy or matter is excited.

The same holds true when you detect a negative vibration. The receiver does not accept this negative vibration, so there is no connection.

When a pure vibration or frequency, free from distortion, is transmitted we call this a signal. When a spurious or false frequency is transmitted we call this noise. Meaningful information is the signal and background noise is unwanted.

The signal to noise ratio is a measure used to quantify how much a signal has been corrupted by noise.

Have you ever had to listen to a radio station while on hold that was not tuned in to the proper frequency? You probably heard more static than you did signal. Did that signal to noise ratio make you want to hang up the phone? Did the "noise" interfere with the "signal" of appropriate music?

If you feel invigorated, refreshed, or encouraged when you are around someone, then they are transmitting a pure signal of good vibrations. Regardless of their physical appearance, their good vibrations attract you to them. Likewise, if you come in contact with a person and you feel aggravated, drained, and discouraged, then they are transmitting spurious noise. Regardless of their physical appearance, their negative vibrations repel you from them.

Perhaps you have noticed that when you are positive people tend to gravitate toward you and your day goes smoothly. Yet when you are negative just the opposite occurs. It is simple to understand.

Just like a battery that has a negative and a positive side—one pulls and one gives, yet both are energy—SO DO HUMANS! And all of us thrive on positive energy!!!

Because this is not a book on physics, I am going to turn your attention away from technical information. I want to demystify frequencies into something you can put to use.

Unfortunately, much of what is available about frequency, resonance, vibration, or energy is shrouded in weirdness. Believe me, what can be accomplished with accurate use of frequency and resonance is nothing short of miraculous. You will soon discover that it is ANYTHING but spooky or weird.

All of this and so much more is but a fraction of God's elemental design for His entire creation. Simply put, it's how things work. Things always get weird when people place their focus on the effect instead of the cause.

"They traded the truth about God for a lie. So they worshiped and served the things God created instead of the Creator himself, who is worthy of eternal praise! Amen."
† Romans 1:25 NLT

What sets this material apart from many others is that I am committed to offer a common sense approach to an uncommon subject. In doing so, I present it sans the overt bend toward eastern mysticism or western fanaticism.

And for the Christian convinced that this type of material is evil or New Age, rest assured it is ANYTHING but new. It is the antithesis of evil. In fact, it is the very genus of the Creator's creation.

Now that we have removed the "freak" from frequency, let's move forward with open minds and hearts to another common but powerful use of frequency: your words.

The Weight of Words

Every word you speak has a frequency. You will now discover that frequencies can create and frequencies can destroy.

**"The tongue has the power of life and death,
and those who love it will eat its fruit."**
† Proverbs 18:21

Here is the application: you have the power to speak life or death with your words. My friends, the words you speak today will continue to bear fruit tomorrow, good or bad.

Have you ever had someone say something to you that hurt you so deeply that you felt sick to your stomach? Did you realize years later that those words had negatively affected your life? On the other hand, do you recall a time when someone encouraged you and those words positively altered the course of your life? Words are frequencies and frequencies have power to produce life or death.

This truth should quickly erase the maxim, "Sticks and stones may break my bones but words will never hurt me." Getting hit with sticks or pelted with stones produces far less damage than one hurtful negative word can.

Probably one of the most captivating illustrations of the life and death nature of words as frequency is presented in a book titled, The *Hidden Messages in Water* by Masuro Emoto.[15]

Masuro Emoto presents one of the most captivating illustrations of life and death word frequency. His book, *Hidden Messages in Water*, shows photos of frozen water crystals formed under a microscope while speaking words. When he spoke words like "love, peace, God, or forgiveness," beautiful water crystals formed. Each crystal was as different as a snowflake, depending on the word he spoke. Interestingly enough, when Emoto spoke the words, "Hate, Satan, chaos, or death," disfigured or broken non-crystalline forms appeared.

This is NOT mystical. It is completely practical. Frequency affects matter and water is matter. Now let's go deeper.

Have you ever noticed the more negative things you say about something the worse it gets? Here is an example. "This stupid car is a piece of junk. It is ALWAYS breaking down!" Chances are if you have said this you have the repair bills to prove it! Automobiles are matter, so matter responds to what you say. Let's take it a step further.

How powerful is a thought? Have you ever heard the saying, "Mind over matter?" The reason mind over matter works is because just like words, thoughts are frequencies and frequencies affect matter. Thoughts become things, not every thought obviously, just the ones you believe!

The difference between thinking and believing is knowing. A better term for a belief that you KNOW is true is faith!

"Now faith is the substance of things hoped for, the evidence of things not seen."
† Hebrews 11:1 KJV

Faith is a belief that is so real to you that you treat it as substance before it manifests. The old saying, "Seeing is believing," is not far off the mark. In fact, faith is only the distance from your head to your heart. Your physical eyes in your head tell your brain to believe what they see. But the "eyes" of your heart cause you to believe what you cannot see, and faith is conceived. If you need to see something before you believe it, that is NOT faith. Faith believes in what you do not see. The reward of faith is to see what you believed you would see before it became a physical manifestation.

Photo credits: Masaro Emoto

"Love & Gratitude"   "Evil"

"Truth"   "You Fool"

"Peace"   "You Disgust Me"

Newtonian physics implies that what goes up, must come down and if you can taste it, touch it, or smell it, then it is. Yet quantum physics implies that what goes up might stay up and if you can taste it, touch it, or smell it, then, it may not be! Newtonian physics is dependent upon gravity and absolutes. But quantum physics defies principles of gravity and absolutes. In other words, with classic Newtonian physics, everything is deterministic. But with quantum physics nothing is; it is just a series of probabilities.

With this new understanding of physics, which of the two sounds more like faith to you? Remember, that which is invisible created everything that is visible. We rarely have trouble accepting what we see as reality. Yet, it is what we don't see that we struggle to believe.

Right now you cannot see the power of the words you are reading or the music I have recorded for this project. Yet it is my fervent prayer that you will feel it and in turn it will radically change your life. I will be sharing more on the subject of frequency when we get to the explanation of the *Wholetones* healing frequency music project section of this book.

CHAPTER 5:

Healing

"All things are possible for one who believes."
† *Mark 9:23*

One of the most controversial subjects I can think of is healing. And to be totally honest, nobody really understands how healing occurs.

In the medical world, exhaustive trials test the effectiveness of pharmaceutical drugs. But they have often ended with a placebo (inert sugar pill) outperforming a potent drug. In fact, the placebo in medical trials is effective at least 30% of the time.[16] There have been cases where doctors give children wooden tongue depressors for their warts. They tell them they are "wart sticks" and if they hold the stick on their wart it will disappear. It often does.[17]

Prayer is very powerful. Some people have amazing results. Yet, while a minister may pray for several sick people, some are healed and some are not. Question: do some medicines work? Does prayer work? The answer to both questions is "Yes!"

Here is another interesting fact. People have survived stage 4 cancer without drugs or prayer. Laughing for hours at a time has healed them![18]

**"A joyful heart is good medicine, but a
crushed spirit dries up the bones."**
† Proverbs 17:22

Laughter is obviously a great means for healing, but is it 100% effective? We could list many things that have accompanied miraculous healings, such as dietary change, alternative remedies, fasting, and exercise. Yet NONE of these would work for everyone all of the time.

Before I continue, so as not to be misunderstood, I believe that prayer should always be the first line of defense when dealing with any circumstance. However, if your prayer lacks one essential ingredient, your words may fall to the ground.

I mentioned this amazing ingredient, faith, in the last chapter. So now let me illustrate it again by offering the following accounts of miraculous healings.

**"Jesus turned, and seeing her he said, 'Take
heart, daughter; your faith has made you well.'
And instantly the woman was made well.**
† Matthew 9:22 ESV

Who was this woman, you ask? She was a woman who suffered with an issue of blood for 12 years and had spent all of her money on physicians and yet was still sick. But, she believed that if she could touch the hem of Jesus' robe she would be healed. (Mark 5:28 shows what the woman believed. Remember that reference "528" when we discuss the frequencies later in the book).

"Then he touched their eyes and said, 'According to your faith let it be done to you'"
† *Matthew 9:29*

Blind men received sight by having faith in Jesus!

"Then Jesus said to her, 'O woman, YOUR FAITH
is great; it shall be done for you as you wish.'
And her daughter was healed at once."
† *Matthew 15:28*

"If YOU believe, you will receive whatever you ask for in prayer."
† *Matthew 21:22*

Here is another example. In John chapter 5, there is an account
of a crippled man who sat by the pool of Bethesda for 38 years
hoping to be healed. When Jesus asked him why he was there, the
man gave him a bunch of excuses. But Jesus said, "Get up, pick up
your bed, and walk." Immediately, the man was made well, picked
up his bed, and walked!

Do you see it? The act of getting up was the crippled man's
evidence of faith. If he didn't truly believe, he never would have
walked! Faith without works is dead. Or in other words, faith
without action is inert. Faith walks, faith speaks, and faith can
move mountains. The "action" of faith is YOUR unwavering,
relentless belief in God's supernatural ability. Even to the point that
you accept no other alternative.

You hold in your hand, right now, a tool that has enormous
power. But your response is twofold. First, read this book and

listen to the *Wholetones* healing frequencies. They will open you up to receive healing benefits. Second, act in faith and just believe.

"Everything is possible for one who believes."
† Mark 9:23

Later in this book I will explain why exposure to certain frequencies often produces spontaneous healing in the human body. I will share with you two amazing stories of actual healings that resulted from using the information in this book. Believe me when I say that your faith will increase exponentially. Remember ... only BELIEVE.

CHAPTER 6:

Discovering the Rabbit Hole

In 1996, after a couple of trips abroad and a visit to a warm mineral spring, I became terribly ill. Over a two-week period my weight dropped from 165 pounds to 135 pounds. I became extremely weak and finally visited a general practitioner. My blood test came back normal, even though I had lost 30 pounds. I had zero energy and could hardly get out of bed. But the doctor said there was nothing wrong with me! I then went to an endocrinologist who accused me of being a hypochondriac. After losing another 5 pounds, I went to an infectious disease specialist only to find out, according to yet another blood test, I was the "picture of health!"

Realizing that I could die before doctors discovered what was killing me, I visited my local health food store to pick up some more supplements. One of the clerks turned to me and said, "You have spent a fortune here and you're not improving. I know someone who can help you." Then the young man handed me a business card and said, "Call him, Michael."

That phone call changed my life. The next day I drove to an office park and met a man we will call "James." I can honestly say I had never met anyone like him. James looked deep in my eyes and said, "Let's find out what's wrong with you ... hold out your finger." In a nanosecond, he put a drop of blood from my finger on a slide, placed it on a dark field microscope and turned on a large television screen. Suddenly, we were looking at my blood sample.

For an hour and a half James told me everything about myself with amazing accuracy from one drop of blood. Then he said, "It's a parasite known as a liver fluke. Have you been out of the country recently?" I told James about my recent travels and he replied, "Let's get you better." What happened next blew my mind.

James turned on a machine, hooked a large capacity syringe to a hose and said, "Ozone is the breath of God. It will kill the parasite that's killing you." And even though there appeared to be nothing in the syringe, I trusted James completely. James put a small butterfly needle into my arm and slowly pushed the syringe.

"This may feel strange and you may lose your sight for a few seconds. But don't be afraid. Your vision will clear. The ocular floaters will disappear and you will be on your way to recovery."

I was a little nervous, but he was holding my hand ... when the lights went out! "I can't see anything!" I said. James calmly replied, "I know. Now count to 30 and it will clear. Thirty seconds later I could see perfectly and the floaters were gone.

After a few more of these ozone treatments, I completely recovered, gained my weight back, returned to work, and felt fantastic. God used this precious man whose methods contradicted modern medicine to save my life. My friendship with James is not only a lifetime one, but it became the door to the "rabbit hole."

James had knowledge of resonant frequencies and protocols for healing the body that were nothing short of amazing. One day, he called me and said he wanted to show me his "voice analysis" diagnostic machine. I couldn't get there quick enough.

When I arrived, James told me to take a seat. He held a microphone up to my mouth and told me to say my name and age and then just talk into the mic for a moment. After James sampled my voice, he showed me the readout of my voice on his laptop. What I saw floored me.

Everything about me flashed on the screen: allergies, vitamin deficiencies, mineral levels, past illnesses, and sensitivities. Then, I saw the proof ... "trace amounts of titanium detected on left ring finger" I was shocked! My wife had just replaced my gold wedding band with a new titanium ring for Valentine's Day!

I asked James how the program knew all of this information by simply analyzing my voice. His reply was the missing link I had been looking for.

"Your voice is nothing more than frequencies and everything about you is embedded in them."

It makes sense when people are ill their voice changes; sickness alters their frequencies. Little did I know that my journey down the rabbit hole had only just begun and everything was about to change.

A year after my recovery, James introduced me to a fascinating man named Dr. Leonard Horowitz. Dr. Horowitz has authored several books, including *Healing Codes For the Biological Apocalypse*.[19] After meeting Leonard, I felt that my theories of sound and light and spontaneous healing with music might be far more than just theories. We will discuss these theories in the upcoming chapters.

Only weeks after meeting Dr. Horowitz, I visited my local health food store to pick up some supplies and visit with the young man who had introduced me to James. As we were talking, a woman approached us, apologized for the intrusion, and said she needed to talk with me. The woman was a nurse and said she felt impressed to invite me to meet her employer. We will call him "Dr. Jake." Dr. Jake received a grant to study how resonant frequencies could affect the human body. I couldn't believe my ears! The woman gave me a business card and told me to arrive at the clinic at 12:45 pm the following Tuesday. The rabbit hole was deepening!

The following Tuesday, I arrived at the clinic and quickly realized that the clinic spanned the entire floor of a medical center. After filling out some forms to protect the doctor's confidentiality, I was brought into a large room with a large "Tesla coil" and a few chairs. Moments later, Dr. Jake walked in, shook my hand, and escorted me into a smaller laboratory suite.

Obviously, my first question was about the huge coil I saw in the other room. But, Dr. Jake completely ignored my question and said, "I am so glad you could come! Let me show you something." He led me to a table with a large microscope. In one fluid motion, he took an eyedropper and drew some water from a beaker, placed it on a slide, and put it under the microscope. "Talk to the water," Dr. Jake instructed.

I told him I didn't want to talk to the water and he said, "Very well, look into the eyepiece and I will speak to the water." I gazed into the eyepiece and Dr. Jake said, "My, what a lovely drop of water you are." Instantly, the water formed a beautiful crystal! Shocked, I asked him to do it again and he repeated the procedure with identical results. Then Dr. Jake said, "Now, watch this!" and he said, "I hate you!"

The beautiful crystal shattered like glass. Immediately, I remembered the Scripture:

"The power of life and death is in the tongue."
† Proverbs 18:21

Before I could speak, Dr. Jake said, "You know, Michael, there is only one creation in nature that fills the entire sonic spectrum: Niagara Falls." Again, I remembered another scripture:

"His voice was like the sound of many waters."
† *Ezekiel 43:2*

I was speechless. When I was about to ask Dr. Jake another question, he said, "Same time next Tuesday, Michael?" Tuesday couldn't come fast enough!

The following Tuesday I had a mild case of laryngitis from speaking Sunday morning and Dr. Jake noticed it immediately. "Let's take care of your voice, Michael. Go take a seat in that chair."

The "chair" Dr. Jake pointed to was situated at the base of the large Tesla coil I spoke of earlier. It didn't look altogether safe. I took a seat and Dr. Jake informed me that the procedure might feel a little strange. With that, I felt a light karate chop sensation on my forehead. "Where's it hitting you?" Dr. Jake asked. When I told him, he punched in another number and the sensation moved to my breastbone. After I told him the location again, he punched in one more number and the sensation moved right over my larynx.

"Perfect! Just sit there for 15 minutes and I'll be back."

True to his word, Dr. Jake returned 15 minutes later. He shut off the machine and asked, "How's the voice now?" "It's ... fine!" I replied totally amazed to find that the laryngitis was gone!

Now you are probably wondering, "What were those numbers the Dr. was punching into the computer?" They were frequencies, very specific frequencies.

As you will undoubtedly discover by reading this book and listening to the 7 healing frequencies in *Wholetones*, frequencies have individual characteristics and abilities. And, everything has a resonant frequency.

So when Dr. Jake entered the frequency for the larynx, he calibrated that frequency for the size of my larynx. It resonated and spontaneous healing resulted. Is that so hard to believe? When you speak, your tongue vibrates, creating frequencies that we call words. And words have the power to create life or death.

There is an account in the Bible where Jesus and his disciples were in a boat on the Sea of Galilee (see Mark 4). A terrible storm arose and the disciples feared for their lives, yet Jesus was sleeping. When Jesus' disciples woke Jesus to inform Him that they were in peril, Jesus stood up and spoke to the wind and waves. "Peace, be still." The wind and the waves obeyed His words and were calmed.

Remember, when it comes to transmitting information, everything boils down to signal vs. noise. The more signal you have in a waveform, the purer the signal.

Jesus had zero noise because He was sinless. When He spoke, it was a perfectly clear frequency that always accomplished its purpose.

"Blessed are the pure of heart, for they shall see God!"
† Matthew 5:8

Here's that Scripture I mentioned in the last chapter. Read it until you believe it:

"Truly I tell you, if anyone says to this mountain, 'Go, throw yourself into the sea,' and does not doubt in their heart but believes that what they say will happen, it will be done for them. Therefore I tell you, whatever you ask for in prayer, believe that you have received it, and it will be yours."
† Mark 11:23-24

If you plant an apple seed, then you won't get an orange. You will get what you planted. Apple seeds produce only apples. In the same way, your words will only produce after their kind, good or evil, blessing or cursing.

- If you're always telling everyone that
  you're sick, then you'll be sick.

- If you're always telling everyone you're
  broke, then you will be broke.

- If you tell everyone that all you ever get in the mail are
  bills, then all you will receive in the mail will be bills!

Be intentional with your words, as frequencies are very specific. In other words, say what you mean and mean what you say.

CHAPTER 7:

Digital v. Analog (Bigger is Better)

I f you have ever attended a live concert hall performance of a symphony orchestra, then I don't need to tell you it is a moving experience. Between the natural resonance of the concert hall and the natural frequency of each instrument, it is nothing short of a sonic spectacle one would not soon forget. The same goes for a great live jazz, rock, rhythm and blues, or folk bands. The key word is "live."

When you hit a drum, strum a guitar, or bow a cello, the instrument resonates. As a result, the frequencies create a sound pressure level. When you experience live sound, you can actually feel the music. This is because the sound waves move the air. And if a public address system (PA) is amplifying the music, then the fullness increases. It moves more air around and efficiently disperses sound through the room.

For many years, music was less disposable. The medium for recording was analog tape machines. The medium for duplicating the music was vinyl discs, or records. To this day, discriminating audiophiles will only listen to analog music recorded on vinyl and played through analog equipment. This is for good reason! It is the one true method for capturing the sonic integrity of the music. Let me explain as best I can the difference between an analog signal and a digital signal.

The main difference between analog and digital signals is that an analog signal has no breaks (continuous) and a digital signal is made up of individual points (called discrete or discontinuous).

Physically measured, an analog signal produces a round sine waveform. But a digital signal produces an angular square waveform.[20]

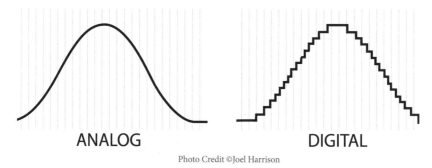

ANALOG   DIGITAL

Photo Credit ©Joel Harrison

The analog sound wave replicates the original sound wave, whereas the digital sound wave only replicates the sampled sections of the original sound wave.[21]

In the recording process, analog technology captures the waveforms as they are. But digital technology samples the analog waveforms and converts them to a limited set of numbers (binary) and records them.[22]

Vinyl records and cassette tapes are examples of analog signals. CDs and Mp3 files are examples of digital signals. In layman's terms, the analog signal is full (big) and organic, while the digital signal is compressed and artificial.

So, why tolerate digital technology? In a word: convenience.

For those of us old enough to remember the excitement of unwrapping your first record player on Christmas, this chapter will resonate with you immediately. But for our younger readers, it may take a bit more convincing.

Vinyl records sound amazing, but they required gentle care and considerable room for storage. So in 1966, the market introduced the 8-track tape. The Ford Motor Company was the first to offer a "cutting edge" 8-track player in their '66 Mustang. By 1970, most Americans had an 8-track player in their homes. Records quickly became less profitable to manufacture because 8-track players were smaller and easier to transport and store.

Within 5 years, the cassette tape offered more convenience and versatility than the 8-track tape. The end of the 8-track started in earnest and the manufacturer's profits started to dwindle.

Just like the record, the cassette tape was still an analog form of media and produced better sound than the vinyl. Then in 1982, Sony released the first compact disc (CD) in America. The CD was the first digital media created to record music. Billy Joel's album, 52nd Street, was the first compact disc release.[23]

The darling of music lovers for a quarter century, the compact disc is finally going the way of the cassette and 8-track. Its size, the advent of stream audio, and digital storage has collapsed the CD industry. The CD will undoubtedly no longer be profitable to the manufacturer.

As you can see, the progress over the last 48 years has merely been in the name of convenience and storage. It certainly wasn't in the name of sonic fidelity. Here is the most interesting phenomenon: people have become accustomed to an emulated sound. It is the media of our day. If manufacturers keep telling the public that smaller is better and the new always outperforms the old, then the next generation of musicians will never know that there is no sound comparison with digital to analog!

Years ago I was playing in a club in Burlington, VT, and a kid came in bragging about his new 200-watt digital guitar amplifier. He boasted how it would blow my old Marshall 50 watt tube amplifier off the stage. So, I decided to teach the youngster a lesson in physics.

The kid brought in his amplifier and set it up next to mine. I told him to "let 'er rip" and he played for a couple of minutes and it sounded all right. But as soon as the band joined in you could not hear the 200-watt digital amplifier at all!

The young man said, "Alright, you play." With the band giving it all they had, my 50-watt analog tube amplifier screamed above the band, much to the shock of that young man. He kept asking, "How is that possible?" I told him to put his hand in front of my speakers when I played. To his amazement, he could feel air blowing out of my speakers.

I gave him a hug and explained to him that a tube amplifier has a push/pull type of transformer. This causes the speaker diaphragm to move in and out and project sound waves. The digital conversion amplifiers, however, do not move the speakers at all. Even though they have a higher wattage rating, they only imitate the sound of the speakers moving. They don't actually move. The recording output label on his amplifier had him convinced: speaker simulator. Now I will convince you!

I know your iPod sounds great to you. But what are you comparing it to? It may be small enough to disappear in your shirt pocket. It may hold 3,000 songs. It may be convenient, portable, and easy to use. But it is filled with über-zipped, truncated, digital music files. Do you really think it would compare to a vinyl record played through a McIntosh tube amplifier into a pair of AR speakers driven by a Bang and Olefson turntable?

There is no question that analog sounds better! However, digital has become the future and all of us, to one degree or another, are forced to use what is readily available.

I like to use the term "social distortion" in reference to the latest digital music mastering techniques. If you think about it, social distortion is an oxymoron to an audiophile.

Growing up in the music industry, we used to brag about releasing projects that were high fidelity with minimum THD (total harmonic distortion), resulting in a cleaner sound. Today, people are into low fidelity and high THD. When it comes to mastering the final mix, obscene levels of compression squash the signal to boost the volume to absurd broadcast levels. In essence, the industry has created a volume war. This gives the artist's music an unfavorable signal to noise ratio. In other words, we listen to loud, distorted tracks.

To add insult to injury, these distorted tracks are listened to on phones or iPods with earphones or cheesy 2-inch laptop speakers! When a major artist invests 500K to record a sonic masterpiece in the studio, what is the point of listening to it through digital junk? Sadly, in our attempts to improve technology we lose integrity.

My purpose is not to criticize digital equipment or digital technology. It is literally impossible to live in today's world without using it. But I simply want to make you aware of truths that you may not be aware of. I dedicate this book to those truths.

One obvious truth is music deserves to be heard with all of the sonic integrity the artist puts into it. With that being said, I want you to know that this *Wholetones* music project was recorded live. The instruments used were primarily acoustic. My electric guitar was played through a tube amplifier and everywhere it was possible, I applied analog technology.

CHAPTER 8:
Sound & Light

"Honey, can you warm up my dinner in the microwave?"

"96 ROCK is my absolute favorite radio station."

"I am scheduled for an MRI tomorrow."

"The doctor said I needed laser surgery to remove this mole."

"My graduating class loved my speech."

"Purple is my favorite color."

"A sunlamp helps me overcome depression during dark winter months."

At first glance, the above statements appear unrelated and random. That could be no further from the truth! The subject matter in each statement refers to frequencies. Microwave, laser, speech, radio station, MRI, the color purple, and sunlamp are ALL examples of frequencies. There is nothing bizarre or unusual about any of these subjects. But when we talk about frequencies that heal, it is suddenly perceived as mysterious or strange.

Have you ever heard of a Gamma Knife? A Gamma Knife isn't a knife at all. Instead, it has a "ray" of light, or focused frequency, and not a blade. Doctors have successfully used a Gamma Knife on over 300,000 patients to remove brain tumors or abnormalities that were otherwise inoperable.[24] It is safe, effective, and non-invasive. The success rate of the Gamma Knife is amazing.

Using frequencies to heal the body is not only practical, but it is quite successful! I predict with great confidence that the use of controlled frequencies for a myriad of applications is the wave of the future. For those reading this and experiencing the *Wholetones* seven healing frequencies, the future is now.

As a child, one of my favorite experiences in elementary school was "show and tell." Every Friday morning, the students would bring something to show and tell to class. Each student called upon would stand before the class, show what they had brought, and tell the class about it. This audio/visual style of presentation was very effective with young minds. Seeing the object stimulated those who learned by sight while hearing about the subject matter instructed the auditory students.

"Ears to hear and eyes to see-both are gifts from The Lord."
† *Proverbs 20:12 NLT*

Sound and light both are frequencies, yet they manifest differently. One is audible while the other is visible. But is that always an accurate litmus test for our human faculties? The answer is a resounding "No!"

To grasp possibilities that we can neither hear nor see, it is essential we understand the truth that frequencies heal. I will do my best to explain this in terms and examples that are easy to understand and utilize.

Regarding sound, we must first realize the human ear can access only a fraction of the frequency range of the entire audio spectrum. Humans hear frequencies from 20 Hz-20 KHz (20-20,000 Hz), which are approximately 10 octaves.

To illustrate this point, consider the "silent" dog whistle. It is silent to us, but certainly not to dogs! Dog whistles range between 23 KHz-54 KHz, well outside the range of human hearing. Whales, dolphins, and bats are capable of hearing frequencies in excess of 100 KHz, which we call the ultrasonic range. And moles and elephants perceive low frequency sounds far below our 20 Hz cutoff point. To be honest, our hearing is quite limited when compared to the totality of audible frequencies.

It is easy to see how our human pride resembles Mr. Owl, mascot of the Tootsie Roll Pop. In the candy commercials, he licks three times then impatiently takes a bite to get to the center. When asked how many licks it takes to get to the center of a tootsie pop, he pompously answers, "Three!"

Often, our human pride keeps us from seeing the big picture. Rather than patiently taking the time to get to the heart of the matter (center of the Tootsie Roll Pop), we chomp it off, losing the benefit of discovering the process. If you believe that what you can hear is all that exists to be heard, you have been lulled into a slumber of denial and I am here to awaken you!

Here is a question to ponder. What happens when we exhaust the audio realm? When we have reached the highest frequency of sound and there is nothing left to be heard, what happens next? We move into a higher frequency realm known as light!

In typical modern polyphony, one octave is 7 notes in an ascending scale. The 8th note is the octave or "tonic" that starts the next scale sequence one octave higher. As higher and higher octaves are achieved, we eventually run out of sound and move into octaves of light. Each time the octave is raised in the audio realm, the "hue" of the note changes but not the note itself. The same holds true in the visual realm.

Each time a color is raised to its next octave, the hue changes. For example, if you add an octave of light to the color forest green, then the color will still be green, but just a different hue. This continues until all hues of color are exhausted and nothing remains but brilliant pure white light!

The Bible tells us there is One who is shrouded by pure unapproachable light: God Almighty! It is impossible for us to fully grasp the concept of an undefiled, spotless, or incorruptible God because we are obviously flawed as humans. So God sent His "unapproachable" light into the world through His son Jesus. He was to be "approached" by man, but also reproached by man. Eventually, the ones He came to love crucified him. In doing so, a spotless lamb was slain for the sins of the world and anyone who would receive Him as Lord would be filled with the same light (frequency).

> "When Jesus spoke again to the people, he said, 'I am the light of the world. Whoever follows me will never walk in darkness, but will have the light of life.'"
> † John 8:12

> "You are the light of the world--like a city on a hilltop that cannot be hidden."
> † Matthew 5:14 NLT

Imagine the power of walking in the same frequency as Jesus! Is it any wonder we read,

"In Him we live & move & have our being."
† Acts 17:28

"Everything is possible for one who believes."
† Mark 9:23

If you have Him, then you have everything. If you don't have Jesus, then you have nothing.

Now here is something to give serious and careful thought to. Just like there are audio frequencies that our ears can't hear, there are also light frequencies that our eyes can't see! In fact, radio waves, microwaves, infrared waves, and x-rays are assaulting you in the air right now. But you can't see a single one of them! At the same time, the dental technician puts a lead apron on you to x-ray your teeth and leaves the room!

My final point here is simple. We have only experienced a fraction of the frequencies of sound and light. Our inability to see or hear them has zero bearing on their reality.

CHAPTER 9:
The Genesis of Music

What is music? What is love? What is light? What is frequency? At the core there remains only one possible conclusion ... GOD!

"Every good and perfect gift is from above, coming down from the Father of the heavenly lights, who does not change like shifting shadows."
† James 1:17

"And God said, 'Let there be light and there was light.'"
† Genesis 1:3

To illustrate my point I will reference something I said earlier, "Let there be light ... " was uttered on the first day of creation. Yet God did not create the sun, moon, and the stars until the fourth day. This makes it quite obvious that HE IS the source of light!

It is important to realize that there is only one source of the many manifestations of frequencies. That one source is the "Father of Lights." This Father gives wonderful gifts to man, as evidenced in James 1:17. In this chapter, we will focus on the gift of music.

In order to understand music, we will have to think of its organic beginning:

- A babbling brook

- A songbird's tune

- A baby's cry

- A child's laughter

- The ocean's roar

- A gentle rain

- Wind through trees

- The crackle of fire

- The rhythm of a heartbeat

All these are the first strains of God's symphony.

The earliest instruments were created in an attempt to contact the Creator. There were no notes or scales, no tuners or key signatures. Drums were made to mimic the sound of thunder that early man assumed was God's voice.[25] Then before long, wind instruments like flutes were created from bird bones to contact the Creator, whose voice they mused was in the wind![26]

The word "muse" means to think about something carefully or thoughtfully. The word "music" means to think using sound. So

Man thought that he could speak to God with sound. The original intention of music is pure: to communicate with God.

As music evolved through the ages, there was still no common ability to fine tune instruments. Some believe the Mesopotamians created structured tunings by 500 BC, but this has not been proven. All we know is that early music had little structure, yet possessed plenty of power. There is considerable documentation that validates this point.[27] I will talk about this later.

Now, I would like to highlight an extraordinary band of monks who employed the greatest instrument of all: the human voice.

The Gregorian chant is the oldest musical manifestation of the Western world.[28] Its roots are steeped in the music of the Jewish synagogues since the time of Jesus Christ and before in the days of King David. The early Christians and disciples of Jesus continued to sing the psalms of the Old Testament. These psalms penned by King David became the inspiration of the Gregorian chants or Solfege (sight singing).

As a teenager, I was introduced to Solfege while training to become a Madrigal singer. Although Madrigal singing is polyphonic and Gregorian chants are monophonic, they both employ interval singing by sight instead of musical notation.

For centuries, the Catholic church considered Gregorian chant its official music. Musical notation for chants of this time did not exist.[29] At the time, chants were an entirely oral tradition, rather than written. Because Christians were persecuted, their private times of worship did not allow for any written examples of music. Then in 313 AD, the "Edict Of Milan" gave Christians the right of freedom of worship in Rome.

The freedom Christianity enjoyed allowed more formalized and organized music to follow suit. It is important to know that 1st century Christianity was referred to as a sect called "The Followers of the Way." Its followers were known as "believers." The term "Christian" was not even used until roughly 40 AD when Paul and

Barnabas taught in Antioch (Acts 11:26). This community started by followers of "The Way" became known as "Christians."

In fact, Antioch became part of the Pentarchy—the universal rule of the five major episcopal jurisdictions over all of Christendom—many years later. It was a major center of early Christianity, founded by the apostles and looked to by their respective regions as leaders in Church life.

When we realize the Roman State Church evolved from 1st century "Followers of the Way," it is easy to understand why it grew quickly.[30] Some of the founding members were relatives who were present on the Day of Pentecost (Acts 2) and the Church was full of life, power and yes … miracles!

What resembles a revival was taking place in the early Roman Catholic Church until the late 500s. Unfortunately, the movements of man eventually curtail true moves of God. Studying church history, you will realize that the further the church veered from Pentecost, the further it strayed from God's divinity. Instead, it became ruled by man's depravity.

The Day the Music Died

As I mentioned, from the Day of Pentecost until the late 500s AD there was a genuine move of God in the early church. Music was the one notable component. Although the music was derived from the ancient monophonic vocal style, it was obviously NOT called Gregorian chant. Gregorian chant takes it name from Pope St. Gregory the Great, who came into power in 590 AD.

It is also important to note this music had its roots in ancient Israel, not Rome, Greece, Italy, or England![31] The early church music quickly drew quite a following. There are historical reports of miracles, outbursts of weeping, rapturous joy, and peace that accompanied the worship.

This would eventually become the official music of the early Roman Catholic Church.[32a] There is a popular saying, "If it's not broken, don't try to fix it," but in 590 AD the newly elected Pope, Gregory the Great, did just that. Historians reported that the Pope reduced the multiple original intervals of the scale to just 7, then modified the ancient music accordingly.[32b] He compiled the altered chants in two books, Antiphonarium and Gradual Romanum, but never actually composed a single chant himself.[33]

No one knows exactly why Pope Gregory decided to revise the intervals of the music and alter its frequencies. I can only imagine the effect and frustration of the vocalists. They had memorized and sung these Solfeggios in unison for years.

Now Pope Gregory told the vocalists what they would sing. He even went as far as to demand that they sing The Alleluia during mass for one entire year!

The theories for why Pope Gregory might have sabotaged the Church's worship are quite plausible. Some believe that Pope Gregory became jealous of the vocalists. They were given notoriety due to the palpable presence of God when they sang.

Others believed it was because Pope Gregory was a collector of religious relics or icons. He believed that the icons possessed great power and that the palpable presence that manifested when the vocalists sang could upstage the relics.

The explanation of why Pope Gregory revised the original Solfeggio tones is interesting. The Church hierarchy said that the intervals (frequencies) were too Holy for the ears of man.[34] It sounds familiar, doesn't it? In the 1500s, a monk named Martin Luther translated the entire Latin Bible into German. For years, the Church told the common man that he could not interpret the Bible. Thanks to Luther, the people could finally read it for themselves. Martin Luther believed the Bible was for everyone and I believe God's gift of music is no different!

Even more shocking is the early church naming the music after Pope Gregory. Ironic, since he is the same one who revised and changed the original intent of church music. His name became synonymous with Gregorian chant. To add insult to injury, we know Pope Gregory today as the patron saint of musicians.

It's a hard pill to swallow if you think about it. God gives miraculous music to man and the church revises it so no one else can hear it the way it was. They thought it was too holy for man!

The chant underwent several reforms and evolutions over time. It was assimilated depending on the practices of the Church, the whim of each new Pope, agendas of monastic orders, and the influence of intermingled cultures such as the Franks, Romans, and Byzantines. By the year 1050 AD, the Church admitted to losing 152 of the original Solfeggios sung by the early Church prior to Pope Gregory.

Along with those Solfeggios, 6 intervals or frequencies inspired by ancient Hebraic songs were also missing, seemingly forever. Some historians believe the Roman Catholic Church burned all the ancient manuscripts.[35] Others believe they are hidden in the archives of the Vatican library. Regardless of what happened to them, what matters now is that those 6 Solfeggio tones, and one ancient "key" that I believe may have been the lynch-pin that inspired 3 of the 6 solfeggio tones, now rest safely in your hands!

CHAPTER 10:
The Six Solfeggio Tones

W hat do the numbers 396, 417, 528, 639, 741, and 852 have in common? They are all numbers, as well as frequencies, like an FM station. Each one has a different characteristic that is seen, heard, and felt.

From a mathematical standpoint, they have another commonality. Look what happens to our frequencies when you apply the skein of Pythagoros, an ancient digital root method that adds up digits until only one number remains, to the numbers 3, 6, and 9.

$$396 = 3+9+6 = 18 = 1+8 = (9)$$
$$417 = 4+1+7 = 12 = 1+2 = (3)$$
$$528 = 5+2+8 = 15 = 1+5 = (6)$$
$$639 = 6+3+9 = 18 = 1+8 = (9)$$
$$741 = 7+4+1 = 12 = 1+2 = (3)$$
$$852 = 8+5+2 = 15 = 1+5 = (6)$$

Now add the numbers in parenthesis only.

9+3+6+9+3+6 = 36 = 3+6 = (9)

"If you only knew the magnificence of the 3, 6 & 9, then you would have a key to the universe."

NIKOLA TESLA (1856–1943)
https://en.wikipedia.org/wiki/Nikola_Tesla

If mathematics isn't your forte, maybe the following photos taken by Masaro Emoto will help you see what I am trying to explain with words.

Photo credits: Masaro Emoto

"D" (Re) 417Mh = 3   "C" (DO) 396Mh = 9

"F" (Fa) 639Mh = 9   "E" (Mi) 528Mh = 6

"A" (La) 852Mh = 6   "G" (Sol) 741Mh = 3

As you can see, water responds to frequencies with beautiful results. Your body, which is composed of 65-75% water, will also respond to these frequencies with beautiful results, even down to the cellular level.

Let's briefly look at each of the 6 Solfeggio tones to understand their individual characteristics.

396 Hz ~ The Open Door

I like to refer to this one as the opening frequency. Most people feel a sense of peace, well-being, and an openness to receive from God when listening.

This frequency has an amazing side-effect: defense mechanisms are arrested and feelings of fear, guilt, and shame subside.

Remember, guilt and shame are not attributes of God. In fact, the Bible says that ALL who look to Him will be radiant and will NEVER feel ashamed.

On a physiological level, this frequency has a positive effect on the blood, liver function, bones, brain function (neuro-transmission), and kidney function.

The corresponding color of this frequency is deep red or garnet.

417 Hz ~ Desert Sojourn

Due to our frenzied schedules and overworking, we often find ourselves stuck in negative cycles. We procrastinate at home, self-medicate with drugs or alcohol, eat junk food on the run, or in other words ... keep bad habits.

This frequency can help break these negative cycles, as well as sluggishness and lethargy.

On a physiological level, this frequency may have a positive effect on the large intestine, enzyme production and the digestive process, stomach, metabolism, prostate, gallbladder weakness, headache due to diet, and lower back problems.

The corresponding color of this frequency is bright red.

528 Hz ~ Transformation

No frequency has received more attention from the fields of science and medicine than 528 Hz ... and for good reason. The 528 Hz frequency has been proven to restore broken DNA, the source of dis-ease.[36]

It is also effective in improving telomere length, which has become a hot topic as of late. As we age, telomeres begin to shorten. If your telomeres get longer, then your life is probably going to get longer, and you're going to have a lower risk of developing a wide variety of conditions. Scientific research is currently underway to see if 528 Hz could have a positive effect on stem cells, as well.

Obviously, if 528 Hz affects DNA, then it would be good for the entire body. It has other noteworthy specific effects on the body that will thrill our female readers. It may help balance hormones, pelvic issues, premenstrual syndrome, pre-menopause, muscle tension, pericardium heart muscle, weight problems, lymphatic, and circulation issues.

Is it any wonder that 528 Hz has been named the Miracle Frequency or Transformation Tone?

The corresponding color for this frequency is a bright green, almost chartreuse.

639 Hz ~ The Bridge

Have you ever found yourself at odds with a friend or loved one? No matter what you said, there was still a chasm of indifference between you and them.

I call 639 Hz The Bridge because it seems to foster a place of forgiveness in our hearts that helps us get over ourselves and make peace with one another.

On a physiological level, 639 Hz may be effective for the endocrine system, especially the adrenal glands, as well as gallbladder issues.

The corresponding color for this frequency is blue.

741 Hz ~ Great Awakening

Most listeners (myself included) found that this frequency has a profound effect on the emotions.

It might bring you to tears, not sorrow, but cleansing tears and an awareness of one's spiritual life. I call this frequency the Great Awakening. In a word, 741 Hz helps awaken us to what transcends our preoccupation with our body and soul and allows us to focus on our Spirit.

From a physiological standpoint, 741 Hz may improve thymus function, bolster the immune system, cleanse from infection (viral, bacterial, and fungal), soothe an upset stomach, and improve function of pancreas, heart, blood and circulatory system.

The corresponding color of this frequency is indigo.

852 Hz ~ The Majestic

There is a famous hymn, "Turn Your Eyes Upon Jesus" by Helen H. Lemmel. The song's chorus best exemplifies this frequency to me.

"Turn your eyes upon Jesus, look full in His wonderful face and the things of earth will grow strangely dim in the light of His glory and grace."
—Helen H. Lemmel (1863-1961)

856 Hz is a celebration of the King of Kings, His love for mankind, and His returning for those who wait for Him. I call 852 Hz The Majestic and when I listen to it I always imagine the awe of seeing Jesus face to face.

As this frequency appears to be purely spiritual, I have no knowledge of its physiological affect, only its ability to connect us in worship of Him.

The corresponding color of this frequency is royal purple.

If you have spent any time researching these frequencies online, then you have probably noticed that there is a cosmic weirdness attached to the subject. In my opinion, this undermines or cheapens its integrity and relegates these amazing frequencies to fringe groups instead of the masses.

I created the materials you now hold in your hands to share with the whole world. In doing so, I hope to change the world and give glory to the source of all frequencies ... God.

It was also obvious in my research that many websites share the same regurgitated information. They have just rebranded it for themselves. I am doing my best to offer as much fresh insight as possible.

The credit goes to Dr. Joseph Puleo and Dr. Leonard Horowitz, two nouveau-renaissance men if there were any. They found these six frequencies embedded in the "The Great Hymn of John The Baptist" Gregorian chant. Even though these frequencies didn't originate from Gregorian chant, these two men are responsible for the discovery.

So instead of reposting their exhaustive research, I would invite you to read the book that brought this great subject to light:

Healing Codes for the Biological Apocalypse by Dr. Leonard Horowitz and Dr. Joseph S. Puleo. Tetrahedron Publishing Group P.O. Box 2033 Sandpoint, ID 83864

Before I continue, I want to make something crystal clear. This is my opinion on the matter. Although man discovered these frequencies, he certainly DID NOT create them. Therefore, we must honor the Creator and not the created for His unspeakable gifts.

Pride makes us think we know everything while knowing little; humility makes us think we know little while knowing much.

"But those who exalt themselves will be humbled,
and those who humble themselves will be exalted."
† *Matthew 23:12 NLT*

What we know, we know by revelation. That's why sometimes you don't have a clue how you know some of the things you know! I am going to share a simple secret with you that will help you receive revelation from God.

"So I say to you: Ask and it will be given to you; seek and you will find; knock and the door will be opened to you. For everyone who asks receives; the one who seeks finds; and to the one who knocks, the door will be opened."
† *Luke 11: 9-10*

This is amazing … it's an acrostic. All you have to do is:

Ask
Seek
Knock

There are three functions appearing in one word. Just like you are comprised of body, soul, and spirit, you are still … you! Is it really that simple? Just ask God and He will answer you?

"Call to me and I will answer you and tell you great and unsearchable things you do not know."
† *Jeremiah 33:3*

The answer is really that easy! If you want to know more, just A.S.K. Now, here's something I bet you didn't know. Count the number of letters in the words, ask, seek, and knock. What did you get? If you answered 12, then you're correct. But, we're not finished. Now apply the number 12 to the skein of Pythagoras:

12 = 1+2 = (3)

Not impressed yet? Add up the numbers of Luke 11:9-10. What did you get? You are correct if you answered 30. But, we're not finished yet. Apply the number 30 to the skein of Pythagoras:

30 = 3+0 = (3)

Don't forget our last scripture, Jeremiah 33:3. Add them up. If you answered 36, then you are correct. But, we're not finished.
Apply the number 36 to the skein of Pythagoras:

36 = 3+6 = (9)
Remember …

"If you only knew the magnificence of the 3, 6 and 9, then you would have a key to the universe." —Nikola Tesla

God IS this magnificence. He IS the key and the numbers 3, 6 and 9 are an integral part of His sequence of creation.

Here is some food for thought. The human body has 639 skeletal muscles that create our ability to move. Doesn't that number sound familiar? God's math always adds UP!

And speaking of adding up, we still have one more very important frequency to talk about. I'd also like you to meet the man I believe is historically responsible for discovering the first 4 Solfeggio tones.

CHAPTER 11:

The Key of David

On my second trip to Israel, my friend Don and I stopped at a coffee house on Ben Yehuda Street on a hunch. You see, Don felt God was telling him to wait at this coffee house because a dear friend of his, who lived in Israel, was going to meet him there. What made this so exciting is that his friend lived in another city and had absolutely no idea that Don was in Israel!

As we waited, I couldn't help notice that the piano player in the corner of the room was smiling and staring at me as he played. He stared so much that I was a bit uncomfortable. I closed my eyes and intently listened to the music of the piano player. I started smiling and whispered to Don, "This guy is a believer. He is playing instrumental versions of Christian worship songs." When I looked at the pianist again, he was still smiling. Looking at me, he nodded his head as if he had heard what I had whispered to Don. As soon as the pianist finished his last song, he made a beeline to our table. Simultaneously, Don's friend Reuven, walked through the door!

What happened next would prove to be the missing link to my understanding of the seventh frequency and a whole lot more.

"You're a believer, aren't you?" the piano player asked. He appeared ready to burst from excitement.

"Yes I am. My name is Michael, and yours?"

"David," he replied. I said, "Of course it is!"

If there was ever a surreal moment, this was it! Don was hugging his friend who God told to get in his car and drive to Jerusalem for a divine encounter with an old friend. And I was sitting with a piano player named David.

David said he knew I was a believer as soon as I walked in. What he was about to tell me, he said I would understand. Before I let him speak, I asked him how he got away with playing Christian songs in a coffee house owned by orthodox Jews. He smiled and said, "It's instrumental music. They don't have a clue that it's Christian. They just love the music."

Since David's break was almost over, he wanted to know if I could stay until his next break. It was imperative I stay because he had something very important to give me. Obviously, it was an offer I could not refuse.

I couldn't help but chuckle as I listened to David playing Christian music in a Jewish Orthodox coffee house. But soon my laughter turned to tears as I saw this musical missionary for who he was: a psalmist, a voice and a gift from God. I was humbled just to be there.

When David finished playing, he said he needed to get something out of his car and he would be right back. When he returned, he sat down and told me that his life's work was studying the psalms of David, an ancient Hebraic form of music. He handed me manuscript copies of several of David's psalms ... I wept.

With tears in his eyes, David said, "These are for you ... Yeshua said you would know what to do with them."

As I stared at one of the manuscripts, it was hauntingly familiar. Then, the light of recognition came on. This was the source of ALL the early first century Christian music, having been sung prior to Pope Gregory and his alterations to what became known as Gregorian chant! Everything was there: monophonic tonality represented as intervals, not notation, but ancient Solfege!

When I looked at David's transcriptions, I noticed that he had adapted these manuscripts to play in modern keys, based on the A440 tuning. At the time, it seemed logical.

When it was time to go, I hugged David and thanked him for his priceless gift. To be honest, I was in awe of God and his ability to connect Don with Reuven and me with David in a coffee house thousands of miles from home. Little did I know I was carrying the key to this project in my hand.

When I got back to my home in Florida, I immediately started playing David's adaptations of the psalms. Though they were beautiful, I felt that something was missing. After a couple of weeks, I filed the music and the manuscripts away in my home office. With my busy schedule, it wasn't long before I forgot about my gift from Israel.

Let me digress for a moment. For the better part of my life, the supernatural had always been quite natural to me. I had always known that music held a key to far more than entertainment. I knew that an unseen hand had been guiding me along a road of discovery, plodding one step at a time.

In 1987, shortly after marrying the love of my life, Lillian, I heard music like I had never heard before. It was late one night in our apartment in Chattanooga, Tennessee. Instantly, it brought me to tears. This instrumental music spoke to the core of my being, without uttering a word. There was no definable key, style, or genre. It was freeform and purely otherworldly.

I shook my wife to wake her and asked her if she heard the music. She had this puzzled look on her face. She hadn't heard anything, but knew I had. I threw on my jacket and slippers to protect me from the cold and ran out the front door to see if someone was playing their stereo in the complex.

I heard nothing but the silence of winter and light snow. I climbed back into bed explaining to Lillian that the music I heard was not coming from outside. As I closed my eyes, the music returned. I listened to my band of angels until sleep found me.

Occasionally, without warning, the invisible symphony would fill my evenings. Finally, Lillian and I were staying in a hotel during a concert tour and she began to weep. "I hear it! I can hear it!" We just lay there completely undone as the mysterious music played into the night.

Periodically, we would run into a musician in my travels that would ask us, "You've heard the sound of Heaven, too?" You have to be careful whom you tell. People have a special name for people who hear voices in their head. I can only imagine what they would call people who hear heavenly music. I'd like to call them blessed!

Believe it or not, hearing heavenly music was just the beginning. Before long, I started touring with an amazing musician named Jason Upton. The name of the band was The Key of David!

From that time, people would approach me at venues and say, "The Lord wanted me to give this to you." They would hand me a key, sometimes a whole ring of keys. Some of the keys were shiny and new; others appeared ancient and rusted. But one thing's for sure, KEYS OPEN DOORS ... and mine was about to swing wide open.

One day, while musing about numerical interpretation, I remembered the number 222. Interpreting the number 222 with a Biblical perspective means, "God's sufficiency in the midst of man's insufficiency."[37]

It reminded me of the scripture, Isaiah 22:22, which is where the band The Key of David got their name. The verse is also tattooed on my right shoulder. So, I read it the scripture again for the millionth time.

> "I will place on his shoulder the key to the
> house of David; what he opens no one can shut,
> and what he shuts no one can open."
> † Isaiah 22:22

Was this the final clue to solve the riddle of the manuscripts that David gave me years ago in Israel? Before I tell you the answer, let me clarify something about Old Testament prophecy.

Often, but not always, there is a "now" and a "not yet" interpretation. This is a double application for a specific Scripture. For Isaiah 22:22, the Scripture is referring to Eliakim son of Hilkiah. A prophet is telling Eliakim that he will take authority over the physical house or palace of King David once the former steward, Shebna, is removed. A key that opens and shuts the palace door will signify the transfer of power.

Eliakim's promise has been fulfilled already, which is the "now" application. Let me offer a possible "not yet" and "then" application that applies to King David and his lineage.[38]

For all eternity, there will be someone in David's bloodline to sit on the throne, with the final King being Jesus.

As a side-note, I'd like to brag on God. As I was writing this chapter, I became overwhelmed with responsibility of providing scriptural fact and theory about King David. I paused for a moment to pray for confirmation and revelation. As I finished, the thought flashed into my mind, "I wonder what appears on page 222 of my Bible?"

Page 222 will be different for each one of us depending on the Bible version and type size you use. I happened to find this on page 222 of the New International Version thinline edition in front of me.

"Obed, the father of Jesse, and Jesse the father of David."
† Ruth 4:22

There is something astounding about David's bloodline, more than I have the wisdom to explain. God made an amazing promise: David's line would NEVER die out. He would always have someone in his bloodline qualified to sit on the throne!

"For thus says the LORD: 'David shall never lack a man to sit on the throne of the house of Israel, and the Levitical priests shall never lack a man in my presence to offer burnt offerings, to burn grain offerings, and to make sacrifices forever.'
† Jeremiah 33:17-18

On the face of it, this seems to suggest that the dynasty of David and the Levitical priesthood would never die out. However, we know that there is currently no king on David's throne (although Jesus is coming to claim it) and there are currently no Levites offering sacrifices.

Furthermore, a contemporary prophet said about the dynasty of David:

"And you, O profane wicked one, prince of Israel, whose day has come, the time of your final punishment, thus says the Lord GOD: Remove the turban and take off the crown. Things shall not remain as they are. Exalt that which is low, and bring low that which is exalted. A ruin, ruin, ruin I will make it. This also shall not be, until he comes, the one to whom judgment belongs, and I will give it to him."
† Ezekiel 21:25-27

In other words, there would be no further king of Israel until Messiah came. This suggests that Jeremiah 33:17 should be understood as meaning that David's line would never die out - he would always have a descendant, someone eligible to sit on the throne.

This is true. There were always people of the line of David until Jesus was born, and he now lives forever. Because the statement about Levitical priests is parallel to the one about David, I suggest it means that the Levitical line would never die out—there would always be people of the tribe of Levi, people eligible to offer sacrifices if and when it is appropriate. This is true too. Consider this short post by Rob J. Hyndman, written May 22, 2010, because I feel it explains this promise God made to David perfectly.[39]

"There are people today with the surname Kohn, Cohen, etc., indicating they are descendants of priests (Hebrew "kohen") and of the tribe of Levi." —Rob J. Hyndman

The Isaiah 22:22 scripture has an application that far surpasses Eliakim's stewardship of King David's former palace. It concerns a greater authority.

As I started to focus on David's life and genealogy, I couldn't help but notice the underdog theme that runs throughout. God loves to make "somebody" out of an apparent "nobody." It is God's nature to oppose the proud and give favor to the humble.

It is funny that the locals in Jesus' day had a saying, "Can anything good come out of Nazareth?" Jesus, the Son of God, came out of Nazareth, Bethlehem (House of Bread) to be exact. He was born in a stable, for goodness sake! Out of the humblest environment, a carpenter's son, Jesus, became the King of Kings.

David's story was quite similar. He was the youngest of eight sons and tended his father's sheep until one day the humble shepherd became the King of Israel. An extensive novel could be written on the life of David alone, so let me get to the point.

David knew things that could have only been revealed by divine revelation. Even though he lived almost 1,000 years before Jesus, David accurately prophesied Jesus' exact words and events of his crucifixion. David also prophesies Jesus' resurrection and future reign (see Psalm 22).

After becoming Israel's King, David changed everything concerning music and worship. We will now take time to focus on that.

Up until the reign of David, Mosaic worship was the accepted form. It was focused on sacrifice and protocol. King David, however, instituted a personal, God-focused mix of praise and intimate worship. This celebrated what God has done (praise) and who He is (worship).

He instituted 24-hours a day worship in the temple by courses. Musicians would worship for 4-hour shifts and then the next group would relieve them. King David also employed the finest musicians in Israel, the Levites.

Solomon worked with his father, David, learning the secrets of perhaps the greatest musician of all time. Yet there were three very important musicians who assisted King David in leadership temple worship. These three men were Asaph, Jeduthun, and Heman. You would be hard pressed to find a team more loyal or skilled in all of Israel.

- Asaph's name means "one who gathers" or "collector." He was a seer prophet and was King David's choir director.[40]

- Jeduthun's name means "man of praise." He came from a family of master string musicians. He was King David's music director or chief musician.[41]

- Heman's name means "faithful" or "support." He was King David's lead singer.[42]

When you add Solomon, whose name means "peace" to the mix, you have: A gathering of faithful men of praise who carried peace![43]

Speaking of peace, when an evil spirit tormented King Saul, he would ask the shepherd boy David to come and play before him.

When David played, the evil spirit left King Saul and his peace returned. David's playing was so effective that King Saul asked David's father, Jesse, if David could stay in his service. It is faithfully recorded that whenever an evil spirit tormented King Saul, David would play and the spirit would leave. (1 Samuel 16:23)

Here is the million-dollar question: why? After all, there were many skillful musicians proficient at the lyre. What made David's playing so effective that evil spirits ran for cover when he played?

The first clue is:

**"He is a brave [fearless] man & a war-
rior ... The Lord is with him."**
† *1 Samuel 16:18, emphasis added*

David had no fear because God was with him and loved David's heart. So for starters, David was a man of God with no fear of man or beast and he had a volcanic heart. But that was just the foundation, there was more ... a LOT more.

David's Lyre

Most people assumed David played a harp, when in actuality the instrument he played was a lyre (or kinnor). A harp is a large instrument with a solid base to hold it upright. It is usually played from a seated position.

The lyre (kinnor) dates back to Ur, the Sumerian city in ancient Mesopotamia where Abraham lived and eventually left in search of Canaan.[44]

Because these people were typically nomadic, they created the lyre (kinnor) as a portable alternative to the harp. The Israelites used two types of lyres, the kinnor and the nebel. Both were made to be carried, although there were some versions of the larger nebel that were the size of a harp. These were played only in temple service.

The kinnor was King David's main instrument and rarely left his side. He was known as the King who ruled with a lyre (kinnor), even carrying it with him to war. Hebrew lore said David's lyre (kinnor) was his scepter, as it was never more than an arm's length away from him.[45]

The nebel was only used during worship and temple service, while the kinnor had a more versatile application. The Hebrews carried it in festive celebrations, joyous occasions, and especially praise and worship in the temple service. But it was NEVER used during occasions of mourning.[46] With that in mind, let me take you to an event that will help you understand these amazing instruments.

"By the rivers of Babylon, there we sat down, yes,
we wept, when we remembered Tziyon (Zion).
We hung up our kinnorot (lyres) upon
the willows in the midst thereof.
For there they that carried us away captive required of

us a shir (song); and they that tormented us required of
us simchah, saying, Sing us one of the Shir Tziyon.
How shall we sing Shir Hashem in an ad-
mat nekhar (foreign land)?
If I forget thee, O Yerushalayim, let my yam-
in (right hand) forget [i.e., have paralysis].
If I do not remember thee, let my leshon (tongue)
cleave to the roof of my mouth; if I prefer not Yerushalayim above my rosh simchah (chief joy)"
   † Psalms 137: 1-6 (Orthodox Jewish Bible)

As previously mentioned, it was forbidden to use the kinnor
during occasions of mourning. The Israelites were so heartbroken,
so dismayed, and so hopeless, that they could no longer make
music. Better to hang them up than to dash them down. Better to
hang them on willows than profane them to the service of idols.
So they hung their lyres up on the willow trees, too forlorn to play.

When their Babylonian captors taunted them and asked them
to sing the songs of mirth that the Israelites sang in their homeland,
they told their captors:

"How can we sing our songs of Zion when
we are captives in a foreign land."
   † Psalm 137:4

Now I want you to muse with me a moment. What are willow
trees known for? The Middle Eastern variety had branches that
were long, slender, and pendulous. They were pliable and easily
moved by the wind.

Jewish lore supposes that there were 120 lyres hung in those
willow trees. Because it was a solemn occasion, the Israelites could
not play them. But what if a gust of wind blew off of the river and

through those trees? It would pull down the weight of the hanging harps and give breath to them. The sound of 120 kinnor, with wind rushing through them, would create a haunting minor sound reminiscent of a funeral dirge. No one alive today actually knows what happened that day. This musing is purely hypothetical.

Regardless, something so powerful happened that it struck fear into the hearts of the notoriously brutal Babylonians. Despite having a reputation for killing their captives, the Babylonians did NOT exterminate the Jews. In fact, after the captives repented to God for their idolatry, Cyrus of Persia defeated the Babylonians and released the Israelites to return to their homeland in 536 B.C. Here is a Biblical account of the Israelites' return:

> "When the Lord brought back the captives [who returned] to Zion, we were like those who dream [it seemed so unreal]. Then were our mouths filled with laughter, and our tongues with singing. Then they said among the nations, The Lord has done great things for them. The Lord has done great things for us! We are glad! Turn to freedom our captivity and restore our fortunes, O Lord, as the streams in the South (the Negeb) [are restored by the torrents]. They who sow in tears shall reap in joy and singing. He who goes forth bearing seed and weeping [at needing his precious supply of grain for sowing] shall doubtless come again with rejoicing, bringing his sheaves with him."
> † Psalm 126 NASB, emphasis added

No one knows who wrote Psalm 126. It is merely labeled, "A song of ascents." It is possible that the caravans of pilgrims going up to attend the annual feasts in Jerusalem sang the fifteen psalms known as the Songs of Degrees or Ascents.

But it is equally possible, and my belief, that the title has a peculiar connection with the music or the manner of using it.

The physical meaning of the "songs of ascent" refers to a festive pilgrimage led by worshippers with kinnors going up to (ascending to) Jerusalem. I surmise that the "songs of ascent" lend themselves to being a musical modulation or "ascending tone." Could it be that these psalms were sung on a high "ascendant" musical note?

What we do know is God was with Israel and the kinnor was still an integral part of Israel's worship. Now I will disclose what I believe made King David's kinnor different from all of the previously existing instruments of the day.

Of utmost importance is the fact that God commanded King David to create the instruments for worship. We know that King David used different wood than typically used to build lyres. He chose cedar from Lebanon, which was a sturdier wood with additional benefits. It was impervious to insects, rot, and saltwater. Combined with its beautiful fragrance, cedar wood made a fine choice for an instrument.

We know that King David's son, Solomon, would eventually commission kinnor and nebel construction from almug wood, or red sandalwood. Because the polished almug wood turned the color of garnet, it was more beautiful than King David's instruments. But Solomon's instruments were NOT used in the placement of the Ark of the Covenant or the dedication of Solomon's temple. The musicians used King David's instruments and here is the result.

"All the Levites who were musicians—Asaph,
Heman, Jeduthun and their sons and relatives—
stood on the east side of the altar, dressed in fine
linen and playing cymbals, harps and lyres.
They were accompanied by 120 priests sounding
trumpets. The trumpeters and musicians joined in
UNISON to give praise and thanks to the Lord.

Accompanied by trumpets, cymbals and other instruments, the singers raised their voices in praise to the Lord and sang: 'He is good; His love endures forever.'

Then the temple of the Lord was filled with the cloud, and the priests could not perform their service because of the cloud, for the glory of the Lord filled the temple of God."

† 2 Chronicles 5:12-14

Obviously, David's instruments didn't create the Glory of The Lord. God's glory, His presence, came in response to the worship created for Him. God gave King David clear instructions on how to worship Him. David's style of worship was obedient to God: intimate, relational, festive, and in 4-hour shifts, 24 hours a day. This created worship that was in Spirit and Truth. King Solomon (David's son) followed those instructions to the letter.

Here is another interesting note. Hundreds of years after King David's death, King Jehoida, King Hezekiah, King Josiah, and the Levites NEVER changed, altered, or deviated from the Davidic style of worship (2 Chronicles, Ezra, and Nehemiah).

The last king of Judah was King Zedekiah, who did what was evil in the sight of the Lord (2 Kings 24:19). However, he managed to do at least one thing that was quite remarkable. He helped hide some of King David's articles of worship just prior to the destruction of Solomon's temple in "Ein Zidkiyah," a location unknown to this day.[48]

Here is a list of just a few of the articles that will remain hidden until the appropriate time:

- King David's 1000 lyres (kinnors)

- 7000 harps (nebels)

- The cymbals (zilzalim) handed down to King
  David from Moses of Sinai (Mishnah 9)[49]

If you were paying attention, you just realized that these are the same instruments used for the placement of the Ark of the Covenant and the dedication of Solomon's temple. King Zedekiah feared these instruments falling into the hands of the Chaldeans. First, they didn't want pagans to use them. Second and more important, King David created these instruments for Israel and the return of their Messiah! No one will find them until they are needed again. God made sure of that!

Putting It All Together

Now I am going to put the pieces of the "Key of David" and "David's Lyre" sections together. This will solve our puzzle and the reason why there are 7 solfeggio tones in your package instead of 6.

One night, while rummaging through my office shelves, I came across the transcriptions of David's psalms that my friend from Jerusalem gave me. It reminded me to look at the original manuscript copies in my file cabinet.

As soon as I looked at the first page, everything suddenly clicked!

"Could it really be that simple?" I said aloud.

I always imagined David tuned his kinnor with some derivative of the note "A," which in Western tuning today would be 440 Hz (more on that later). I also knew that David tuned higher than many of his contemporaries. Suddenly, I remembered page 222 in my Bible, as well as Isaiah 22:22. I asked myself, "What if I double them to 444? Could the tuning be 444?"

Then the bomb dropped! Could it be more than a note … maybe a key, THE key of David? There was one only way to find out!

I grabbed my guitar and tuned it to 444 ("A") and there it was: 4 of the 6 solfeggio tones were right under my fingers!

- 396 Hz (which is "G" tuned at 444 Hz)

- 417 Hz (which is "G#" tuned at 444 Hz)

- 528 Hz (which is "C" tuned at 444 Hz)

- 639 Hz (which is "Eb" tuned at 444 Hz)

The transcribed manuscripts from Jerusalem copied in the key of D (440 Hz) didn't work because they were in the wrong key and the wrong tuning. Once I looked at the original manuscript everything lined up. I remembered the words of my piano playing friend David.

"These are for you … Yeshua said you would know what to do with them."

In one night, it was like solving a musical Rubik's cube. It wasn't the Gregorians who discovered the solfeggio tones. It was King David—and he received them from God!

Suddenly, it all made sense. Because David was not satisfied with the kinnors that were available to him, he built his own. He chose cedar from Lebanon because it was a stronger, warmer sounding wood. Cedar has a very warm and beautiful tone, as well as being delightfully aromatic. Its strength holds up under the higher tensile strength of the 10 strings tuned to 444 Hz. Most of my guitars have cedar soundboards because of the exceptional tone. Furthermore, since David's kinnor would need to survive thousands of years, he chose cedar because it is impervious to insects, even termites.

By now, I was pacing as the Holy Spirit answered all the questions in my mind. I began to understand why the "Sound of Heaven" was so elusive and impossible for musicians to capture.

There are two ingredients that determine true worship: Spirit and Truth. The mind and the flesh are not spirit. Human reasoning, as well as raw talent, cannot create that which is spiritual. Music that touches God MUST come from the Spirit.

"But an hour is coming, and now is, when the true worshipers will worship the Father in spirit and truth; for such people the Father seeks to be His worshipers. God is spirit, and those who worship Him must worship in spirit and truth."
† John 4:23-24

Not only have we been playing music in the wrong key, but also we often do it with impure motives. King David was a man after

God's own heart. Though he was flawed as we all are, God loved David's heart!

> **"After removing Saul, he made David their king.
> God testified concerning him: 'I have found Da-
> vid, son of Jesse, a man after my own heart; he
> will do everything I want him to do.'"**
> *† Acts 13:22*

When someone plays music with true spiritual motives and properly directs it to God in worship of HIM alone, God responds and heaven invades earth.

This profound gift of worshiping in Spirit and Truth was passed on through the generations. David taught his son Solomon, along with Asaph, Jeduthun, and Heman, all that God had showed him so that true worship would remain upon the earth … forever!

Through the power of progeny, Asaph, Jeduthun, and Heman were responsible for writing many of the psalms. Solomon wrote several psalms, including The Song of Songs, also known as The Song Of Solomon.

It was David's honor to share his secrets and it is my honor to share mine with you.

CHAPTER 12:

Looney Tunes

Here is a novel question. "Does tuning really make a difference?" My answer would be, "Only if you are interested in spontaneous healing, changing the world, and touching the heart of God."

As I mentioned earlier, early music tuning was inconsistent. There was no standard tuning and tuning equipment had not been invented yet. Here is a website to confirm the facts about what I am about to tell you: www.schillerinstitute.org

As I mentioned in the last chapter, David tuned his kinnor to 444 Hz. However, other musicians of the time did not follow the same standard. Tuning would eventually become stringent due to polyphony and larger symphonic works.

I hope this sheds light on King David's choice for making his lyre (kinnor) out of cedar. He was a man tuning up in a culture that was tuning down.

In the late 1600s through early 1800s, 417 Hz and 432 Hz were popular tunings. From a harmonic standpoint, they were favorable frequencies in regard to the body on a cellular level. We understand why when we apply them to the skein of Pythagoras.

$$417 \text{ Hz} = 4+1+7 = (12) = 1+2 = (3)$$
$$432 \text{ Hz} = 4+3+2 = (9)$$

Joseph Sauveur (1653-1716), the father of musical acoustics, originally influenced J.S. Bach, Beethoven, and Mozart to tune to 432 Hz. Later, Ernst Chladni (1756-1827) defined middle "C" at 256 Hz ("A" 432 Hz) as a scientific pitch. So, we can safely say that "C" 256 Hz or "A" 432 Hz was the dominant tuning of that time.[50] For example, German instruments made during between 1780-1827, including replicas of those instruments, could only be tuned to 432 Hz. Even today, many symphony orchestras still tune to 432 Hz.

In 1815 in Vienna, Czar Alexander demanded raising the pitch to create a "brighter" sound. Although many classical musicians resisted, Friedrich List and Richard Wagner pushed for the higher pitch in the 1830s and 1840s.

By 1850, instruments were redesigned to play at pitches from 420 Hz (A) to 460 Hz (A). Some played even higher in the cultured theaters of Venice. A full swing tuning war thus began in Europe!

Now, let me introduce some exact quotes from the Schiller Institute regarding the politics of tuning:

"In the late 1850's, the French government, under
the influence of a committee of composers led by bel
canto proponent Giacomo Rossini, called for the first
standardization of the pitch in modern times. France
consequently passed a law in 1859 establishing A at
435, the lowest of the ranges of pitches (from A=434 to
A=456) then in common use in France, and the highest
possible pitch at which the soprano register shifts may

be maintained close to their disposition at C=256. It was this French A to which Verdi later referred, in objecting to higher tunings then prevalent in Italy, under which circumstance 'we call A in Rome, what is B-flat in Paris'. Following Verdi's 1884 efforts to institutionalize A=432 in Italy, a British-dominated conference in Vienna in 1885 ruled that no such pitch could be standardized. The French, the New York Metropolitan Opera, and many theaters in Europe and the U.S., continued to maintain their A at 432-435, until World War II."

—SCHILLER INSTITUTE

Now read carefully. Here is where it gets interesting. The shift to 440 Hz tuning became accepted but never standardized in the United States.

"In fact, A=440 has never been the international standard pitch, and the first international conference to impose A=440, which failed, was organized by Nazi Propaganda Minister Joseph Goebbels in 1939. Throughout the seventeenth, eighteenth, and nineteenth centuries, and in fact into the 1940s, all standard U.S. and European textbooks on physics, sound, and music took as a given the 'physical pitch' or 'scientific pitch' of C=256, including Helmholtz's own texts themselves. Figures 13 and 14 show pages from two standard modern American textbooks, a 1931 standard phonetics text, and the official 1944 physics manual of the U.S. War Department, which begin with the standard definition of musical pitch as C=256.

The first effort to institutionalize A=440, in fact, was a conference organized by Joseph Goebbels in 1939, who had standardized A=440 as the official German pitch. Professor

Robert Dussaut of the National Conservatory of Paris told the French press that: 'By September 1938, the Acoustic Committee of Radio Berlin requested the British Standard Association to organize a congress in London to adopt internationally the German Radio tuning of 440 periods'.

This congress did in fact occur in London, a very short time before the war, in May-June 1939. No French composer was invited. The decision to raise the pitch was thus taken without consulting French musicians, and against their will. The Anglo-Nazi agreement, given the outbreak of war, did not last, so that still A=440 did not stick as a standard pitch.

A second congress in London of the International Standardizing Organization met in October 1953, to again attempt to impose A=440 internationally. This conference passed such a resolution; again no Continental musicians who opposed the rise in pitch were invited, and the resolution was widely ignored.

Professor Dussaut of the Paris Conservatory wrote that British instrument makers catering to the U.S. jazz trade, which played at A=440 and above, had demanded the higher pitch, 'and it is shocking to me that our orchestra members and singers should thus be dependent upon jazz players.' A referendum by Professor Dussaut of 23,000 French musicians voted overwhelmingly for A=432.

As recently as 1971, the European Community passed a recommendation calling for the still non-existent international pitch standard. The action was reported in "The Pitch Game," Time magazine, Aug. 9, 1971. The article states that A=440, "this supposedly international standard, is widely ignored." Lower tuning is common, including in Moscow, Time reported, "where orchestras revel in a plushy, warm tone achieved by a larynx-relaxing A=435 cycles," and at a performance in London "a few years ago," British church organs were still tuned a half-tone lower, about A=425, than the visiting Vienna Philharmonic, at A= 450."

—SCHILLER INSTITUTE

Let me fill in the blanks so that regardless of the rhetoric you may hear elsewhere, I want you to know the truth … and the truth will set you free.

The 440 Hz frequency is a dissonant, unrested, and chaotic tuning that creates agitation in the human body.

The next section is a portion of an article written by Dr. Leonard G. Horowitz, DMD, MA, MPH, DMN (Hon.).[51]

Abstract

"This article details events in musical history that are central to understanding and treating modern psychopathology, social aggression, political corruption, genetic dysfunction, and cross-cultural degeneration of traditional values risking life on earth.

This history concerns A=440 Hz "standard tuning," and the Rockefeller Foundation's military commercialization of music.

The monopolization of the music industry features this imposed frequency that is "herding" populations into greater aggression, psychosocial agitation, and emotional distress predisposing people to physical illnesses and financial impositions profiting the agents, agencies, and companies engaged in the monopoly.

Alternatively, the most natural, instinctively attractive, A=444 Hz (C5=528 Hz) frequency that is most vividly displayed botanically has been suppressed. That is, the "good vibrations" that the plant kingdom obviously broadcasts in its greenish-yellow display, remedial to emotional distress, social aggression, and more, has been musically censored.

Thus, a musical revolution is needed to advance world health and peace, and has already begun with musicians retuning their instruments to perform optimally, impact audiences beneficially, and restore integrity to the performing arts and sciences.

Music makers are thus urged to communicate and debate these facts, condemn the militarization of music that has been secretly administered, and retune instruments and voices to frequencies most sustaining and healing."

DR. LEONARD G. HOROWITZ
DMD, MA, MPH, DMN (Hon.)
http://drlenhorowitz.com

Thank you, Dr. Leonard G. Horowitz for your passion and tireless research. You have confirmed that A = 444 Hz is a healing, life giving key. It supports why I am openly exposing A = 440 Hz for what it is: detrimental to the human body.

Now ask yourself this question. Why would Joseph Goebbels, propaganda minister and right hand man to Adolph Hitler, master of mind-control, manipulation, and unspeakable evil, be so concerned with the international standardizing of musical pitch?

Before I answer that question, here are just a few of Joseph Goebbels famous quotes.[52]

"If you tell a lie big enough and keep repeating it, people will eventually come to believe it. The lie can be maintained only for such time as the State can shield the people from the political, economic and/or military consequences of the lie. It thus becomes vitally important for the State to use all of its powers to repress dissent, for the truth is the mortal enemy of the lie, and thus by extension, the truth is the greatest enemy of the State."

"The most brilliant propagandist technique will yield no success unless one fundamental principle is borne in mind constantly - it must confine itself to a few points and repeat them over and over."

"Think of the press as a great keyboard on which the government can play."

"Faith moves mountains, but only knowledge moves them to the right place."

"Intellectual activity is a danger to the building of character."

"If the day should ever come when we [the Nazis] must go, if some day we are compelled to leave the scene of history, we will slam the door so hard that the universe will shake and mankind will stand back in stupefaction."

"Whoever can conquer the street will one day conquer the state, for every form of power politics and any dictatorship-run state has its roots in the street."

JOSEPH GOEBBELS (1897-1945)
https://en.wikipedia.org/wiki/Joseph_Goebbels

Who was Joseph Goebbels? In short, a monster. Let me provide you with brief explanation of Joseph Goebbels' position as a Nazi.

Goebbels was Hitler's Minister for Propaganda and Public Information. He coordinated the Nazis' election campaign that brought Hitler to national power in January of 1933.

Once in control, his goal was to "Nazify" the art and culture of Germany. Accordingly, he ordered all "un-German" books burnt on May 10, 1933.

Goebbels used radio and propaganda films to win over supporters. He was also responsible for creating a cult of personality for Hitler.

In November 1938, it was Goebbels' idea to exploit the murder of a German diplomat in France by a Jewish youth (Herschel Grynszpan) to stage a violent program against the Jews of Germany. He gave this violent outburst its cynical name Kristallnacht.

He turned the Germans against their "enemies" by creating and spreading lies and hatred. He depicted the Jews as sub-human creatures who were the Germans' greatest enemies. Goebbels thought that people would only believe lies if they were repeated often enough. The bigger the lie, the greater the chance it would be believed. During World War II he carried on a personal propaganda blitz to raise hopes on the home front.

Named chancellor in Hitler's will, he remained with Hitler to the end. The day after Hitler's suicide, Goebbels and his wife killed themselves and poisoned their six children.

Is the light bulb coming on yet? Are you seeing any correlation between this mentality and that of today's political agenda? Is it a coincidence that a Nazi, anti-Semitic, outright hater of the Jews would push for a tuning (A = 440 Hz) that facilitates social unrest, agitation, and friction? At the same time, replacing harmonic, life-giving tunings such as 417 Hz, 432 Hz, and especially 444 Hz, which was given to the Israelites (Jews) by God Himself?

I'll pose the question again. Why would Joseph Goebbels, propaganda minister and right hand man to Adolph Hitler, master of mind-control, manipulation, and unspeakable evil be so concerned with the international standardizing of musical pitch?

My answer is control, manipulation, and power.

The good news is, what God has ordained man will NEVER be able to destroy. That includes the Nation of Israel, the key of David, and the TRUTH!

As we approach the end of this book, may it be the beginning of a "musical love revolution" or "res-o-nation" that shifts this world on its axis. The key is within your grasp.

CHAPTER 13:

The Application of Intonation

Here is a statement I would ask you to take to heart. **"Life is too short to live out of tune."** Intonation is simply the accuracy of pitch. For example, if the intonation of a guitar is off when you tune the instrument to a pitch, then it will still be out of tune with itself. Once you calibrate the guitar by correcting the intonation of the bridge, when tuned, the instrument is in tune with itself and resonates properly.

The human body is no different. When the cells of the body are in tune with each other, the body functions flawlessly and resonates with life. When the body is in a state of disease, it is out of tune with itself and in need of cellular intonation.

In the chapter of this book titled Healing, I mentioned people use different modalities to be healed. Yet NONE of them are effective without faith.

Most of you reading this book received it with 7 *Wholetones* music CDs. If you only purchased the book, then I highly recommend that you order the CDs or downloads. They were created to intonate your body. Or simply put, they create the environment for your body to experience spontaneous healing by listening to these God-given frequencies.

Before I recorded the *Wholetones* disc set, I only had my guitar to play healing frequencies. Even so, I received many phone calls and emails with amazing stories of physical healing from when I played. But nothing was medically documented.

That changed in 1995. I was playing guitar in a church in Dayton, Ohio when a man told me to unplug my guitar and play it over a girl seated in the front row. When I unplugged my guitar and walked down the stairs, I remember thinking how bizarre the request sounded. I placed the headstock of my guitar on her abdomen and started to play and she started to weep. After what felt like an eternity, the man said I could return to the stage and we played one last song.

When the service was over, we went to the green room for refreshments. There I asked the man why he had me unplug my guitar and play over the girl. He said, "She's healed!" "From what?" I asked. "Crohn's disease. It's gone!"

Sure enough, two weeks later the man called our ministry to inform us that the girl was healed from Crohn's disease. She has an MRI to prove it! That is when I realized God is God and He can heal any way He wants to.

He can rub mud in a blind eye and open it (John 9). Or He can use the headstock of a guitar to heal a girl with Crohn's disease. Healing is HIS business and I am just honored to be a part of it.

But of all the healings I have seen, none compared to what happened to my mother in 2005. When mom called and told me that they had discovered a mass on her pancreas, I was stunned. Immediately, my wife and I packed our bags and headed across the state to be with her during surgery. They had scheduled the surgery, but due to a mix up at the hospital they postponed the surgery and sent mom home for the night. When we got to mom's condo I remembered that I had brought my guitar with me. I asked mom if I could play my guitar over her. Silly question, my mom loves my guitar playing! She said, "I would love that".

I remembered the girl in Ohio who was healed from Crohn's disease, so I started playing (741Hz). I touched mom's side where her pancreas is located with the headstock of my guitar as I played. After a few minutes, my mom exclaimed, "It's all green, I see green, something is happening". Mom had her eyes closed the entire time I played and I knew that something was happening.

The next day she was back in the hospital being prepped for surgery. The surgeon, a wonderful Christian man, took time to explain the procedure to us, as well as the difficulty and the duration of the surgery. Then he said the most amazing thing, "I only treat them, God heals them." I felt peace for the first time in days!

The staff informed us the surgery should take approximately four hours. The surgery took much, much less time than anticipated and a nurse came to let us know the surgeon would be out to talk to us in about 15 minutes. When the surgeon came out, he rushed down the hall saying, "No cancer! No cancer! I've already heard from pathology and everything came back clear!"

PAMELA JANTOMASO

You can see a video of my mom telling the whole amazing story at our website: www.wholetones.com

At the end of the day, God gets the glory for healing. Without faith, it is impossible to please God.

"And without faith it is impossible to please God, because anyone who comes to him must believe that he exists and that he rewards those who earnestly seek him."
† Hebrews 11:6

God created music and gave it to mankind as a gift. The frequencies recorded onWholetones reflect the integrity of proper intonation and have been known to trigger spontaneous healing in the body.

This is the impetus behind *Wholetones.* To see people healed and to create a global awareness for musicians to recalibrate their tuning from A 440 Hz to A 444 Hz. This would create an environment of healing everywhere when performing music.

Think about it … your life is a musical! Music surrounds you wherever you go: television, radio, the Internet, commercials, sporting events, school, church, phone and even crickets singing.

Those who are wise through the ages have understood the power of music and have used it both for good and for evil. Music is like a hypodermic needle, a perfect vehicle to introduce its content into the human soul. Depending on the content and the motive of those responsible for the music, one of two results is always inevitable:

- Life or death

- Blessing or cursing

- Healing or disease

Which would you prefer?

For this reason, if the marketing and manipulation of music is with dubious motive or greed, it is a detriment to producing life, blessing, and health. The proliferation of properly intonated, selfless, pure, healing music created with love produces life. If adopted on a global scale, then it could ultimately change the world.

There are only two ways one can live life. Either you will live it from the outside in or from the inside out. Period.

A life lived from the outside in is primarily self-centered. The prevailing thought is, "What's in it for me?" It will do whatever it takes to get more.

On the other hand, a life lived from the inside out is aware of the wealth it already possesses. The prevailing thought is, "What can I do for others?" It will do whatever it takes to give what they have away.

People who always take never have enough and people who always give are never in need.

"Jesus himself said, 'It is more blessed to give than to receive.'"
† Acts 20:35

This is the proper direction to live your life. What if the world (ethos) adopted this "pay it forward" lifestyle? One man did and billions have benefited from His benevolence.

"You know about Jesus of Nazareth, whom God anointed with the Holy Spirit and endowed with power. Jesus traveled around doing good and healing everyone oppressed by the devil because God was with him."
† Acts 10:38 NLT

With the information printed here and the healing frequency *Wholetones* music, you have the tools to become a world changer and a history maker. But in the end, will it be for your fame or their freedom?

The choice is yours.

CHAPTER 14:

Nuts & Bolts (How to Use *Wholetones*)

I n our final chapter, I want to explain how to get the most out of your *Wholetones* resources. Before addressing the musicians, let me share some practical information with my non-musical friends.

Unless you skipped to the end, this book has hopefully awakened you to the power of healing frequencies. At the very least, it has challenged you to go deeper in your own research. Awareness is the first step toward discernment. Discernment is the antithesis of ignorance or lack of knowledge.

It is amazing how our minds work. For example, I might ask if you have seen the new Corvette. Your reply might be "No." But the next day if I ask you the same question, your reply would probably be "Yes." Why? Until I mentioned the Corvette, you weren't looking for one. But by asking the question I planted a "seed of awareness." This caused you to look for the Corvette.

This book is also a "seed of awareness." It will cause you to look for the truth. The truth may exist between the rocks or the secret place of the stairs that looms just out of your periphery, beckoning you to search it out.

Sometimes, like God, the truth is fractal. You can only see a fraction of it at a time. Until the day that you realize your image was too small and you zoom out until you are able to see the truth for what it is — magnificent.

Sometimes, like a man with his nose pressed against the Mona Lisa, we are too close to something precious to grasp its value. Not until we back up to take it all in do we realize its worth.

Here is my advice. Try looking at everything and everyone in your life through the wide lens. The beauty you have taken for granted will amaze you. You will become humbled by what you had missed.

After you finish this book, find a quiet place and re-read it again with fresh eyes. This time read it slowly and make it personal. I am sure you will find some buried treasure that you missed the first time.

After reading this book, if it has changed your life or challenged you, then order copies for your friends and family from the website, www.wholetones.com. Even give copies to your enemies; it will make a world of difference in the way they view life. As always, have an extra set of the *Wholetones* CDs and DVDs with you to give to someone in need of healing. The most effective way to spread good news is word of mouth. When each one tells one, a whisper becomes a shout.

Now that we have covered the book, let's talk about the *Wholetones* music.

Using Your Wholetones
Healing Frequency Music

As you examine the CD case (or digital download), you will discover 7 color-coded discs. Each color corresponds with the 7 frequencies used in this recording. Each disc is 22:22 in length and covers one frequency from start to finish.

You can always refer to the "The Six Solfeggio Tones" and "Putting It All Together" chapters of this book to refresh your memory of the characteristics of all 7 frequencies.

Please keep in mind that each track is 22:22 minutes long. If you played all seven frequencies back to back, then that's over two and a half hours of music!

Let the music play continuously in your home to enjoy the most benefit from the CDs. The 7 frequencies, especially 396 Hz and 741 Hz, will calm even the most nervous dog or cat when you're away.

The most therapeutic use of the *Wholetones* CD set is to find the one or ones that are suited to your exact situation. One way to do this is to take the test on the *Wholetones* Facebook page.

Here is another tip. Always start with 396 Hz. It is the Opening frequency for a reason. Then, continue with the specific frequency or frequencies needed for the application.

For example, if I had an upset stomach I would listen to 396 Hz, The Open Door, and follow with 741 Hz, Great Awakening. I would also make sure that there were no distractions for the entire 44:44 minutes.

Some people prefer listening on headphones, which is also quite effective. Noise canceling headphones are also a welcome alternative when you can't escape to a quiet place.

As you can imagine, the applications for healing music are many. Play the frequencies at the hospital, the room of a sick child or loved one, in the car, your office at work, while you sleep,

Bible study, prayer meeting, or during massage therapy. Put them on when the kids are fighting and watch what happens. The sky's the limit!

You will be able to access more resources on our webpage here at www.wholetones.com. Come and read the healing testimonies from others who have benefited from the *Wholetones* books, music CD's, DVD's, and videos from our site in digital or physical format.

For My Music Friends

Now let me address my musician friends who are interested in joining the revolution. Can you guess what is the number one question I am asked by musicians?

"Why can't I figure out the chords to your music?"

And those of you who read my book already know the answer,

"Because you are tuned to A 440 Hz and you can't get here from there!"

People have a hard time grasping the fact that the notes played on the *Wholetones* 7 CDs exist between the notes they are accustomed to in the lifeless 440 Hz tuning.

It should excite you to know when I show you how to tune up in a down tuned generation you will be playing notes that others have never heard. Others may have never known these notes existed.

To access these 7 tones, you will have to tune to A 444 Hz first. That will give you:

- 396 Hz as G

- 417 Hz as G#

- 444 Hz as A

- 528 Hz as C

- To access 639 Hz as Eb, you must tune to Eb at 444 Hz and play E. A guitarist can play open chords here. Otherwise, to reach 639 Hz, instruments will play Eb tuned to A 444 Hz.

- To access 741 Hz, we must for the first time leave our beloved 444 Hz and tune to 441 Hz and play an F# which gives us 741 Hz. Again, if a guitarist wishes to play open chords you would tune to Eb in 441 Hz and play a G.

- To access 852 Hz, tune to 451 Hz and play G# which is 852 Hz. To play open chords, tune to Eb in 451 Hz and play an A.

Musicians have the ability to powerfully touch peoples' lives with their music. Just imagine the impact you will have by altering your tuning a mere 4 musical cents. Change your tuning … change a life … maybe your own!

Maybe you are thinking,

"What about other musicians I play with who tune to 440 Hz?"

Simple, be a musicianary and teach them why it is important to switch from 440 Hz to 444 Hz.

How many musicians do you know who spend a fortune on the latest gear so that they sound better? Nothing will make you sound better than changing your tuning to 444 Hz. It is not difficult at all.

If you are an electric keyboard or synth player, your job is simple, just change your instrument's internal tuning to 444 Hz.

If you are an acoustic piano player, then ask your tuner to calibrate to 444 Hz and play away.

For my guitar-playing friends, you will need a digital tuner that can be calibrated. The easiest one I have found is the Korg CA- 30.

You might want to ask your drummer to do what mine did to record on the *Wholetones* CD project … tune his drums! The Korg CA-30 Tuner will work for daring drummers as well.

Here is one more reason to tune to 444 Hz. It will inspire you to write. As you are playing notes that few others are playing, yours will be refreshing, not sounding like other bands.

Every time you play you will be using ancient tones that bring healing instead of chaos into the world. You will be part of the solution instead of just a continuation of the problem.

Let's start a reformation of Intonation. Help me re-tune the world and release a Sound of Healing that replaces chaos with peace and a revolution of love … for love NEVER fails.

Life is too short to live out of tune. Tune up, tune in, and release the sound of healing everywhere you go. It will make all the difference in the world!

Let me leave you with the chorus from the song, "Did You Hear the Mountains Tremble?" by Delirious.[53]

"Open up the doors and let the music play
Let the streets resound with singing
Songs that bring Your hope
Songs that bring Your joy
Dancers who dance upon injustice
Open up the doors and let the music play
Let the streets resound with singing"

MARTIN JAMES SMITH
Songwriter

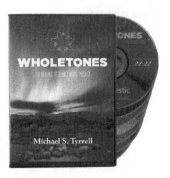

The Healing Frequency
Music Project

Love the Book? Expect to Be Changed! The Healing Frequency Music Project was created to promote positive, healthy change. Seven unique songs recorded in seven unique frequencies on seven CDs results in $2^{1/2}$ hours of beautiful, transformational music. Listeners say that WHOLETONES facilitates spontaneous healing in the body and the music brings a tangible sense of peace that permeates their home. Entrepreneurs have reported increased focus and productivity, leading to breakthrough ideas.

Artists, musicians, and writers are experiencing heightened levels of creativity and vision. WHOLETONES is ideal music for: prayer rooms, hospice care facilities, nursing homes, hospitals, waiting rooms, offices, family counselors, massage therapists, schools, and more.

Order the ground-breaking 7-CD set for a life changing, in-depth journey into the mysteries of frequency healing. *To learn more about and to purchase WHOLETONES: The Healing Frequency Music Project, visit www.wholetones.com today.*

Testimonials

"I play them continuously in my home. It keeps the atmosphere so peaceful. You just have a true sense of well being while listening! My son-in-law is an Iraq war veteran who came home with PTSD as well as some physical injuries. We recently took a cruise with him and my daughter, and we saw that Rick was having great anxiety being around all the people. I had my wholetones loaded on my mp3 player, when I saw Rick getting anxious I gave him my mp3. The soothing music helped him remain calm. My daughter is going to order the wholetones to keep playing them continuously in their home. I am praying they will help him as he also suffers from severe headaches due to a brain aneurysm he suffered on his return from Iraq."
—MARLENE L. ON SUNDAY, FEBRUARY 1ST, 2015

"Desert Sojourn has become my go to lately (listening to it right now). I first noticed when I play it, my knees become warm. I've had sore knees for a long time and lots of bone on bone creakiness, etc. When I play Desert Sojourn not only do I feel heat, but I have increased the ability to do things like squat (which I've been unable to do for years) and have much less pain."

—PATSY V. ON MONDAY, FEBRUARY 9TH, 2015

"A 10 year old boy with autism was found calm upon entering the center after having a rough day at his school. The CD was being played when he entered the center. The staff has found the various CDs to promote the relaxation; settling was needed in an effort to meet the needs of the students. Each appears to be a start for healing and further communication. Michael thanks for using your God given talent."

—JACQUE ON TUESDAY, MARCH 10TH, 2015

Wholetones Chroma

Turn Your Living Room Into A '*Wholetones* Healing Spa' with the Healing Light & Sounds of *Wholetones*.

When you listen to *Wholetones: The Healing Frequency Music Project* your body is bathed in layer after layer of music infused with specially tuned frequencies. Now we've added Chroma™ - a color-balanced and specially tuned video that's a feast for your eyes and body. Each Chroma video disc lets you experience the *Wholetones* frequencies in full. You'll be pulled into the music even deeper with the added benefit of video tuned to the same frequency.

What You Get:

- (1) Blu-ray Disc

- (1) DVD Video Disc

- 2 Hours & 36 Minutes Total Running Time

- High Fidelity Audio Mastered at 48k 24bit

- Option to Play One Video or "Repeat All"

- Enhanced with Chroma (light) Therapy
  Visit www.wholetones.com/chroma to see it for yourself.

Both Discs Include:
- 396 Hz Open Door

- 417 Hz Desert Sojourn

- 444 Hz The Key of David

- 528 Hz Transformation

- 639 Hz The Bridge

- 741 Hz Great Awakening

- 852 Hz The Majestic

- How to Use Chroma

Chroma Testimonials

"*Wholetones*, and Michael Tyrrell's latest work "Chroma," which incorporates chromatherapy, are regular staples at the Hansa Center. In fact, we are using Chroma in two treatment rooms now. It is a masterful work!"

DR. DAVID JERNIGAN
Nationally recognized as a leader in Biological Medicine and the treatment of chronic illness at The Hansa Center.
http://hansacenter.com

"Chroma is illuminating and energizing our grow room. It is awesome!!!"

JORDAN RUBIN
Founder of Beyond Organic & Author of The Makers Diet
http://www.makersdiet.com/

"As medical science breakthroughs are occurring at the speed of light, yesterday's science fiction is today's science fact. Chroma light therapy helps me keep my energy flowing freely for vitality and a sense of wellbeing."

DR. SHINO BAY AGUILERA
Board Certified Dermatologist & Dermatologic Surgeon, Physician Trainer & Clinical Researcher

Acknowledgements

Eighteen years have come and gone since I first began to conceptualize this project. Over that span of time, countless numbers of personalities have left an imprint upon my soul. It would be virtually impossible to thank everyone who has inspired me or helped me along the way, so please forgive me if your name does not appear in print. That being said, there are people who have invested time, expertise, resources, love, prayer, encouragement, and life to the *Wholetones* project and to me! So it is with love and gratitude that I mention the following:

God: For giving me breath and length of days.

My amazing wife, Lillian: Thank you for believing without seeing and loving without measure; I love you, more!

Mom: Thank you for giving me life, teaching me truth and making me who I am today; I love you.

Dad (Pat): For loving everyone and never giving up on anyone!

My sister Tammy: You are a shining star and your love moves mountains; I love you.

To Alvaro & Elizabeth Bazurto: Thank you for your love, prayers, and for Lillian!

Alex Bazurto: For friendship & amazing ability to understand me.

To my dear friends, Joe & Amanda Barton: Thank you for helping make this dream a reality … from scribbles on a napkin to a book and music that changes lives; you are amazing!

Cheryl Ravey: Thank you for your editing prowess and devotion to this project.

Leslie Prins: Thank you for making the videos pop and tying up loose ends at the finish line!

The entire Barton Publishing staff: It takes great people to make great things happen. Thank you.

Joel Harrison: Nobody else could have made the graphic design match the beauty of the book and the *Wholetones* music; you, sir, ROCK; love you!

Richard Aronson: My friend … your videos, virtue, and vibes are epic. Thank you for investing in me.

James Johnson: Sonic guru and dear friend, thank you for your blood, sweat, and tears. The *Wholetones* tracks are heavenly.

Sundui Chimidkhorloo, Dustin Horne, Coty Sloan, & Steve Morgan: Your love, devotion, and musical excellence in the recording of *Wholetones* "Healing Frequency Music Project," brought Heaven to Earth; thank you.

Mike & Patti Coleman: Thank you for being born! Your friendship is oxygen … We will celebrate soon!

Rick Pino: We have traveled roads both broad and narrow; may we meet soon at another intersection! Bless you.

Brian "Head" Welch: You are a gem. Your friendship and the life you shine are priceless … you are changing the world. Thank you.

Kirk Gilchrist: Thank you for all you do for so many; your vision inspires me. You have a friend for life.

Don Finto: Thank you for being a father and a lover of Israel; your investment in my life is reaping big dividends.

Dr. Shino Bay Aguilera: Words cannot express my gratitude for all you have done for me and so many others … I cherish our friendship. Thank you!

Vick & Katha Nelson (and family): Rare are the times in life when you meet people that capture your heart and walk with you through anything. You have literally changed my life and I love all of you more than words can describe.

Joel & Amy Nelson: We are family! Your love for me is humbling; thank you for everything. Your honesty, brilliance, love, and scientific analysis helped me write this book with accuracy, honesty, and integrity. Love you.

Marti Fouce: We are inseparable … your gift of wisdom, love, and generosity are life changing. We have laughed and cried together; it's time to laugh again and celebrate life. Thank you.

Barry Otto: You, sir, are amazing! Thank you for all you've done for me … arrrrr!

Dr. Dan Proeschel: Everyone talks about how white my teeth are and it's all your fault! Thank you for your friendship and belief in what I am doing. God bless you.

Jim Brown: You, my friend, saved my life. God has used you and Eric to open my eyes to a myriad of modalities to restore health and walk in faith and I can never thank you enough.

Big Bob & Michele Ladendorf (and family): Throughout the years, our friendship has only gotten stronger! Thank you for believing in me; this is a BIG year for both of us … love you all.

Ron McConaughey: Thank you for making my travels around this big blue marble so much easier … you are the best!

Special Thanks

The Network Gang (Mike Moss, Mike & Cheryl Ravey, and Mylena Jubenville), Asa & Shelly Hilliard, Raya Williams, Grace Feng Hsu, James & Kim Maultsby (and family), The Rodriguez Clan, The Oakridge Gang, John & Cynde McClain, David Guilliams, Chris & Jennifer Hopper, Mike & Linda Smith, Arlene Tierce, Bob & Patty Barton, Howard & Jennifer Newman, Sheila & Don and everyone at Don Fredericks, Michael & Leslie Shew, Steve Bliss, Dr. Leonard Horowitz, and of course, Zivah.

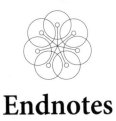

Endnotes

The Game Changers

1. Greatsite Marketing. "English Bible History, Martin Luther." greatsite.com. Accessed September 8, 2014. http://www.greatsite.com/timeline-english-bible-history/martin-luther.html

2. Flynn, Paulie. "Leonardo Da Vinci's Inventions." leonardodavincisinventions.com. Accessed September 8, 2014. http://www.leonardodavincisinventions.com

3. Knox, Dr. E.L. Skip. " History of the Idea of Renaissance." europeanhistory.boisestate.edu. Accessed September 8, 2014. http://europeanhistory.boisestate.edu/latemiddleages/renaissance/historyren.shtml

4. Wheeler, Dr. L. Kip Wheeler. "The Chain of Being: Tillyard in a Nutshell." web.cn.edu. Accessed September 8, 2014. https://web.cn.edu/kwheeler/Tillyard01.html

5. Livingston, Dr. David. "Was Adam a Caveman?" davelivingston. com. Accessed September 8, 2014. http://davelivingston.com/ adamcaveman.htm

6. Perissinotti, Frank. "History of Architecture, Renaissance Architecture." St. Clair College, Windsor, Ontario, Canada. Accessed September 8, 2014. http://www.stclaircollege.ca/people/ pages/fperissinotti/arc300ge/week6/week6.html

7. "Renaissance." The Free Dictionary. 2009. Accessed September 8, 2014.http://www.thefreedictionary.com/renaissance

Proximity vs. Perspective

8. Nichols, Lacy. "What Are Linear & Nonlinear Thinkers?" ehow.com. Last modified April 17, 2014. http://www.ehow.com/ info_8656021_linear-nonlinear-thinkers.html

9. Rudolf the Red-Nosed Reindeer, Directed by Larry Roemer. 1964. New York, NY Rankin/Bass Productions [us], 2000. DVD.

Time & Eternity

10. Jesus, Dinosaurs and More. "The Bible and Radiometric dating (The Problem with Carbon 14 and other dating methods)." dinosaursinthebible.com. Accessed September 8, 2014. http:// www.angelfire.com/mi/dinosaurs/carbondating.html

11. Gascoigne, Bamber, Peter Donebauer, Ian Henghes, Steve Jelley and Sir Kit McMahon. "History Of The Calendar." historyworld. net. Accessed September 8, 2014. http://www.historyworld.net/ wrldhis/PlainTextHistories.asp?historyid=ac06

12. Foss, Sam. "The Calf-Path." poets.org. Accessed September 8, 2014. http://www.poets.org/poetsorg/poem/calf-path

Freakquency or Frequency
13. Kortegaard, Bert. "What is resonance or resonant frequencies?" Yahoo.com. Accessed September 8, 2014. https://answers.yahoo.com/question/index?qid=20090304122744AAHhQrJ

14. Wilson, Brian. Good Vibrations. Los Angeles: Capital Music Group. 1966. www.sing365.com/music/lyric.nsf/Good-Vibrations-lyrics-Beach-Boys/0B8C6AE2E060D42A48256985000 2441C

15. Emoto, Masuro. The Hidden Messages in Water. New York, NY: Atria Books. 2005

Healing

16. Faith Brynie, PhD, "The Placebo Effect: How it Works," Psychology Today, January 10, 2012

17. Tyrrell, Michael. "Faith to See Your Healing." Barton Publishing. Last modified July 28, 2014. http://www.homecuresthatwork.com/columns/spiritual-dimension-of-wellness/faith-to-see-your-healing/#.VA4fj0uxUWY

18. McGhee, Dr. Paul, "Use Your Amuse System to Boost Your Immune System." LaughterRemedy.com. Accessed September 8, 2014. http://www.laughterremedy.com/articles/immune_system.html

Discovering The Rabbit Hole

19. Horowitz, Dr. Leonard. Healing Codes For the Biological Apocalypse. Las Vegas, NV: Healthy World Distribution. 1999.

Digital Vs. Analog (Bigger Is Better)

20. PreSonus Audio Electronics, Inc. "Digital Audio Basics: Sample Rate and Bit Depth." presonus.com. Accessed September 8, 2014. http://www.presonus.com/community/Learn/sample-rate-and-bit-depth

21. Goldman, Jonathan. "The Sound of Light." healingsoundsblog. com. Accessed September 8, 2014. http://healingsoundsblog. com/2008/10/06/the-sound-of-light/

22. Deruty, Emmanuel. "Dynamic Range & The Loudness War." SOS Publications Group. Accessed September 8, 2014. http://www. soundonsound.com/sos/sep11/articles/loudness.htm

23. Giles, Jeff. "30 Years Ago: The First Compact Disc Released." Loudwire Network. Accessed September 8, 2014. http:// ultimateclassicrock.com/the-first-compact-disc-released/

Sound & Light

24. Penn Medicine. "The Penn Gamma Knife® Center at Pennsylvania Hospital." pennmedicine.org. Accessed September 8, 2014. http://www.pennmedicine.org/neuro/gammaknife/

The Genesis of Music

25. Kaili, Du. "From thunder to battle, temple to tower: the origin and legacy of the Chinese drum." Chinese Social Sciences Today.

Last modified March 3, 2013. http://www.csstoday.net/ywpd/Features/52925.html

26. Welsh, Jennifer. "Caveman Flutists? First Instruments Date Back 40,000 Years." purch.com. Last modified May 24, 2012. http://www.livescience.com/20563-ancient-bone-flute.html
27. Flutopedia. "Flutes of Gilgamesh and Ancient Mesopotamia." Manifest Spirit Music. Last modified August 31, 2014. http://flutopedia.com/mesopotamian_flutes.htm

28. McGraw-Hill Higher Education. "The Humanistic Tradition, Volume I, Music Listening Guides, Chapter 5." highered.mheducation.com. Accessed September 8, 2014 http://highered.mheducation.com/sites/dl/free/0073523976/812959/fiero6_musiclistening_v1.doc.

29. Wikipedia. "Gregorian chant." wikipedia.org. Accessed September 8, 2014. http://en.wikipedia.org/wiki/Gregorian_chant Wikipedia. "History of Christianity." wikipedia.org. Accessed September 8, 2014. http://en.wikipedia.org/wiki/History_of_Christianity

30. McGraw-Hill Higher Education. "The Humanistic Tradition, Volume I, Music Listening Guides, Chapter 5." highered.mheducation.com. Accessed September 8, 2014 http://highered.mheducation.com/sites/dl/free/0073523976/812959/fiero6_musiclistening_v1.doc.

32a. Wikipedia. "Gregorian Chant." wikipedia.org. Accessed September 8, 2014. http://en.wikipedia.org/wiki/Gregorian_chant

32b. Anonymous (1841, July-December). Church Music, The Christian Remembrancer: A Monthly Magazine and Review, Vol. II, 192 retrieved from https://books.google.com/books?id= hw8EAAAAQAAJ&pg=PA192&lpg=PA192&dq= Antiphonarium+gregory&source=bl&ots=0zIoFnICal&sig= GsfWQOL2KYNeGeoxQ5smZLDg9Gg&hl=en&sa=X&ved= 0CCUQ6AEwAWoVChMIzoOuzL_JxwIVhCceCh3toQGp#v= onepage&q=Antiphonarium%20gregory&f=false

33. Wyatt, E. G. P. "St. Gregory and the Gregorian music." archive. org. Accessed September 8, 2014. http://archive.org/stream/ stgregorygregori00wyatuoft/stgregorygregori00wyatuoft_djvu.txt

34. "Healing Codes for the Biological Apocalypse" by Dr. Leonard Horowitz, p. 345-6

35. Mowry, Scott. "LIFE TRANSFORMATIONAL TOOLS #9: The Ancient Solfeggio Frequencies – The Perfect Circle of Sound." miraclesandinspiration.com. Accessed September 8, 2014. http:// www.miraclesandinspiration.com/solfeggiofrequencies.html

The Six Solfeggio Tones

36. Anderson, Vicky. "Resonance." hiddenlighthouse.wordpress. com. Last modified October 14, 2014. hiddenlighthouse.wordpress. com/tag/dna/

The Key of David

37. Flaws, Jack. "God Counts." Straight Talk about God. Accessed September 8, 2014. http://asis.com/~stag/godcount.html

38. The Dwelling. "The Key of David." 24-7worship.org. Accessed September 8, 2014. http://www.24-7worship.org/pb/wp_343368ee/wp_343368ee.html

39. Bible hub. "623. Asaph." Biblos.com. Accessed September 8, 2014. http://bibleq.net/answer/2575/

40. Bible hub. "623. Asaph." Biblos.com. Accessed September 8, 2014. http://biblehub.com/hebrew/623.htm

41. Bible hub. "Jeduthun." Biblos.com. Accessed September 8, 2014. http://biblehub.com/topical/j/jeduthun.htm

42. Bible hub. "1968. Heman." Biblos.com. Accessed September 8, 2014. http://biblehub.com/hebrew/1968.htm

43. Bible hub. "Solomon." Biblos.com. Accessed September 8, 2014. http://biblehub.com/topical/s/solomon.htm

44. Levy, Michael. "Composer for Lyre." ancientlyre.com. Accessed September 8, 2014. http://www.ancientlyre.com/historical_research/

45. Mindel, Nissan. "The Complete Story of Shavuot." Kehot Publication Society. Accessed September 8, 2014. http://www.chabad.org/library/article_cdo/aid/2049/jewish/The-Shepherd-Who-Became-King.htm

46. Levy, Michael. "Composer for Lyre." ancientlyre.com. Accessed September 8, 2014. http://www.ancientlyre.com/the_biblical_kinnor/

47. Salem Web Network. "Theology of Chronicles." biblestudytools.com. Accessed September 8, 2014. http://www.biblestudytools.com/dictionaries/bakers-evangelical-dictionary/chronicles-theology-of.html

48. Mock, Robert D MD. "The Prophet Jeremiah and the Five Guardians of Solomon's Temple Treasures, Part Eleven." biblesearchers.com. Accessed September 8, 2014. http://www.biblesearchers.com/temples/jeremiah11.shtml

49. Lexi Line. "The Valley of the King(s)." lexiline.com. Accessed September 8, 2014. http://www.lexiline.com/lexiline/lexi80.htm

Looney Tunes

50. FIDELIO Magazine, Volume I, No. 1, Winter 1991-92

51. Horowitz, Leonard G., Dmd, Ma, Mph, Dnm (Hon.). "Musical Cult Control: The Rockefeller Foundation's War On Consciousness Through The Imposition of A=440hz Standard Tuning." medicalveritas.org. Accessed September 8, 2014. http://www.medicalveritas.org/MedicalVeritas/Musical_Cult_Control.html

52. Goodreads Inc. "Joseph Goebbels quotes." goodreads.com. Accessed September 8, 2014. http://www.goodreads.com/author/quotes/281832.Joseph_Goebbels

Nuts & Bolts ~ How to Use *Wholetones*

53. Smith, Martin James. Do you hear the mountains tremble? Brentwood, TN: Sparrow Records. 2009. http://www.delirious.org.uk/document.php?id=907

About the Author

Michael S. Tyrrell, is an Author, speaker, ordained minister, musicologist, musician, composer, and producer. With over thirty years of experience in the music industry alone, he has shared the stage and the studio with a virtual, "who's who" of well-known musicians. His work earned a Grammy in the mid-eighties. As an ordained minister, Michael has served as a youth pastor, associate pastor and worship leader in Nashville, Tennessee, and North Lauderdale, Florida. Michael currently travels internationally as a sought after keynote speaker and worship leader and is the president of "The Network Center," a non-profit organization that exists to connect and encourage like-minded believers, churches and ministers for greater global impact. As an author, Michael's non-linear thinking and multifaceted knowledge of various topics creates a fresh approach to his writing style. Michael had previously been known for his insightful blogs and Road Journals, which he wrote while traveling as a touring musician. In recent years, his articles as a staff writer for Barton Publishing's internationally acclaimed health and wellness publication, *Home Cures That Work*, created the demand for this book.

Over the years, Michael had been asked on numerous occasions to write a book and his reply was always the same, "I will write a book when I have something to say, books that become timeless have a purpose … never write a book because you can, write a book because it's needed." Michael has carried the seed for this, his first book, *Wholetones: The Sound Of Healing*, for 18 years and after you sample its "fruit" you decide if this book was needed.

In the 60's, troubadours like Bob Dylan carried more than music; they had a message for a generation. In his second edition of this book, *The Sound Of Healing: Unveiling the Phenomena of Wholetones*, Michael S. Tyrrell has penned a clarion call to his generation. As an author, Michael possesses an uncanny ability to create pictures with words that draw the reader into deep places of enlightenment and personal introspection. People that have read his published works often commented that they felt as though he was writing to them personally. Blessed with an innate ability to "demystify" the mysterious and explain the inexplicable, he communicates in a way that even a child could appreciate.

Michael lives in South Florida with his wife, Lillian, and their beloved dog, Zivah.